THE JEWISH PEOPLE
A PICTORIAL HISTORY

THE JEWISH PEOPLE
A PICTORIAL HISTORY

LEON AMIEL PUBLISHER
New York–Paris

KETER PUBLISHING HOUSE JERUSALEM LTD.

Design and Layout—Shlomo Barlev
Execution—David Oren

Published in the Western Hemisphere by
LEON AMIEL PUBLISHER
New York–Paris

ISBN 0-8148-0609-0
Library of Congress Catalogue Card Number 74-12590

Distributed in the rest of the world by
KETER PUBLISHING HOUSE JERUSALEM LTD.
P.O. Box 7145, Jerusalem, Israel

ISBN 0-7065-1464-5
Catalogue Number 25645

Set, printed and bound by Keterpress Enterprises, Jerusalem
Printed in Israel

Contents

1

B.C.E.	2000			1900
EGYPT		X I I	D Y N A S T Y	
3rd Ur Dynasty collapses	M A R I	M I D D L E	B R O N Z E	A G E

1
The Hebrews
Early Origins (2000 B.C.E.—1250 B.C.E.)

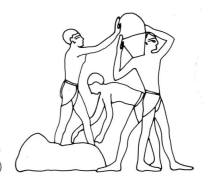

Jewish history began about 4000 years ago in Mesopotamia. Recent archaeological evidence has lifted some of the mist enveloping human affairs during that period, and has revealed that the Mesopotamian area (which roughly comprises modern Iraq) was the cradle of many later civilizations and the center from which various peoples migrated to other parts of the Middle East. It was there too, according to the biblical account, that Abraham received God's command to take his family to Canaan, the land which the Almighty promised would belong to his descendants. Abraham migrated south-westwards along the Fertile Crescent, and it is from his origin beyond (*me'ever*) the River Euphrates that the name "The Hebrew" is derived. But Abraham did not only father a semi-nomadic group: he founded a new religion. His rejection of paganism, and his belief in the One Unseen, All-Powerful God, became the first principle of later Judaism. The practice of circumcision ("the covenant of Abraham our father") became the first duty of all male Jews.

In Canaan, Abraham led a pastoral and secluded life. His only recorded purchase of property was the Cave of Machpelah, which later became the family tomb. Of Abraham's two sons, the elder Ishmael (born to Hagar) later became the father of the Arab people. It was the younger son, Isaac (born to Sarah), who continued his father's religious beliefs. The son, no less than the father, displayed complete faith in the Almighty when he was even prepared to obey a divine command to sacrifice Isaac. Only at the last minute did God order Abraham to stay his hand.

Isaac's twin sons, Esau and Jacob, were from an early age intense rivals, fighting for their father's birthright and his blessing. Ultimately Jacob tricked his brother out of both. But so great was Esau's consequent anger that Jacob had to seek refuge with his uncle in Mesopotamia, and did not return to Canaan for 21 years. By that time he had taken four wives and had one daughter and 12 sons. It was from the latter that the Twelve Tribes were later descended. By divine command, Jacob had also adopted the alternative name of Israel.

Jacob's family preserved its uniqueness in Canaan, refusing to assimilate with surrounding pagan tribes. But this did not prevent a degree of internal friction. In particular, Jacob's favoritism towards Joseph, his eleventh son, gave rise to jealousy amongst the other brothers. They conspired to sell Joseph into slavery in Egypt. Despite several vicissitudes, Joseph prospered in Egypt, ultimately becoming viceroy to Pharaoh. He also saved his family. When the region was stricken by famine Joseph, who had taken timely measures to cope with the disaster, arranged for his father and brothers to settle in the Egyptian province of Goshen. But the prosperity and honor which Jacob's family enjoyed in Goshen were short-lived. After the death of Joseph, a change of ruler occurred in Egypt and brought a reaction against the Israelites (as we may now call them). They were reduced to the status of slaves and subjected to a series of repressive measures.

The movement for liberation was led by Moses, an Israelite who had been raised in the royal household but who had been forced to flee to Midian as a result of his activities on behalf of his brethren. There God commanded him to lead the Israelites out of Egypt. Moses was confronted by both the stubborn opposition of Pharaoh and the sullen reluctance of his brethren. Only after ten catastrophic plagues had befallen Egypt was God's command fulfilled. Not until the miraculous destruction of the Egyptian army in the Red Sea was the Israelites' redemption complete. In Jewish history the Exodus from Egypt constitutes the supreme symbol of the legacy of freedom, and one never to be forgotten. The people which had itself experienced oppression was forbidden to mistreat other unfortunates. The Israelites were also enjoined to commemorate their redemption by the annual feast of Passover.

7

אל־אברם
אליעזר
וְהָבֵ
אלֵי

3

עבורה־זרה

4

8

5

6

7

8

9

10

10

Motif: Egyptian brickmaking in the 15th century B.C.E.—the period of the Israelite bondage—depicted in a fresco in the tomb of Rekhmire (18th dynasty) at Thebes.

1. Typifying the Middle Eastern idolatry which Abraham rejected is this bronze figurine of the contemporary Canaanite goddess Asherah, cast from a Middle Bronze Age mold recently found in a seaside temple at Nahariyyah.

2. Hathor, a gilded bronze goddess dating from the Late Bronze Age (1550–1200 B.C.E.), is a relic of Egyptian idolatry during the period of the bondage. It was found at Bet She'an (in Israel) which was then under Egyptian rule.

3. The binding of Isaac (Gen. 22:1–19); mosaic in sixth-century synagogue at Bet Alpha.

4. Canaanite child sacrifice; a boy led to the pyre of the god Moloch in 18th-century copperplate engraving by M. Richey.

5. Abraham's hospitality to his three angelic visitors (Gen. 18); medieval mosaic in the Basilica of S. Maria Maggiore in Rome.

6. "The Sacrifice of Isaac;" oil painting by Giovanni Guardi.

7. Pharaoh's portentous dream of the seven cows (Gen. 41); ivory panel from the sixth-century "Throne of Maximian" in Ravenna.

8. The Mer-ne-ptah stele, Thebes, c. 1230 B.C.E. Line 27 reads: "Israel is laid waste, his seed is not."

9. Joseph drawn from the pit (Gen. 37:28); window in St. Stephen's Cathedral in Vienna.

10. Semitic nomads entering Egypt; tomb painting at Beni Hasan, dating from c. 1890 B.C.E., during the patriarchal period.

11. "The Finding of Moses" (Ex. 2:5–6); oil by Paolo Veronese.

12. Moses with Jethro's flock approaches the burning bush (Ex. 3:1–2); illumination in *Sarajevo Haggadah,* 14th century, Spain.

13. Moses by the burning bush (Ex. 3:5); mural in the third-century synagogue at Dura-Europos near the Euphrates.

ΤΟΘΕΟΒ · · ΔΙΑΓΩΝ · · ΟΡΩ

2
From People to Nation
Conquest of the Land (1250 B.C.E.—1150 B.C.E.)

The motley collection of slaves who escaped from Egypt did not immediately enter Canaan. Initially directed into the wilderness by God, they later feared a trial of strength with the powerful inhabitants of the land. This lack of faith brought stern retribution. With only two exceptions, none of those born into slavery ever entered the Promised Land. Instead, they continued to wander in the wilderness of Sinai for 40 years until the last generation of slaves had died.

The central event of their passage through the wilderness was the Revelation. It was at Mount Sinai—the exact location of which is disputed—that the Pentateuch (Torah) was transmitted to the people and there that God himself spoke the Ten Commandments to the assembled Israelites. He commanded them henceforth to be a holy people and a nation of priests. The difficulty of fulfilling this aspiration was immediately apparent. Within forty days of hearing the divine command not to construct any graven image, the people had begun to worship a golden calf. On a subsequent occasion they even begged to return to Egypt. Only the personal intervention of Moses prevented divine retribution.

Moses, indeed, is the central figure of the epoch. He alone communicated with God "face to face," and he alone welded the disjointed rabble into a recognizable people. He was at once military leader, administrator, and legislator. The crowning tragedy of his life was that he too was forbidden entry into the the Promised Land. The crowning achievement, however, was his promulgation of the series of divine enactments. The latter have remained the foundation of Jewish practice and jurisprudence to our day. They have also inspired much of the humanitarian idealism of modern times.

The settlement of the Land of Canaan began under Moses' successor, Joshua. Commencing from the base which two and a half of the tribes had already established on the eastern bank of the Jordan, the Israelites gradually spread across the country. The conquest was a slow and laborious process, only occasionally speeded by divine intervention. While the capture of Jericho, for instance, was swift, costless and miraculous, it was not for many generations that the invaders were able to subdue the Philistines on the coast. Some tribes, unable to establish a permanent foothold in the land, continued to lead a semi-nomadic life. Joshua's arrangements for the division of the land amongst the tribes was in effect more theoretical than practical.

Moreover, the tribal confederation forged in the desert proved to be a loose affair in Canaan. The former wandering shepherds had settled down as peasants, tradesmen, and merchants. The unity of common experience was now replaced by diverse and rival concerns. Despite the vague national feeling fostered by the common religious cult, the Israelites lacked even a rudimentary unifying constitution. Instead, after Joshua, leadership was vested in a sporadic series of judges. Some of these leaders did successfully combine the functions of elder and commander. Under the direction of Deborah, Ehud, Gideon and Jephthah, the Israelites won some modicum of peace and security. But not even these leaders were able to unite the tribes. Neither were they able to ensure the constant adherence of the Israelites to the national religion, nor to establish a central shrine for the monotheistic cult. The Book of Judges depicts the period as one in which the people alternated between the worship of the true God, and paganism.

The circumstance of intense local jealousy sometimes facilitated foreign invasion. The tribes were constantly subject to attack from the Canaanites and their allies, and in only a few cases of real emergency did they successfully combine against the common foe. During this period even internecine warfare amongst the tribes was not unknown. That of Benjamin, for instance, was almost annihilated by the others for refusing to agree to the punishment of the recalcitrant town of Gibeah. The fact that the Israelites did survive this crucial period of their history must not be allowed to conceal the difficulties which they experienced in doing so.

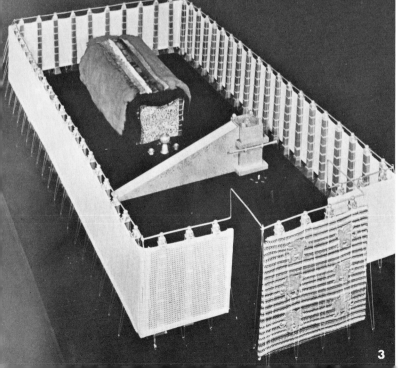

Motif: Moses brings the Decalogue (Ex. 32:15) to the waiting Children of Israel, who are wearing medieval Jewish hats; miniature from an illuminated Hebrew manuscript, France, c. 1280.

1. Moses receives the Law (Ex. 19:20) on Mt. Sinai, at the foot of which St. Catherine's Monastery already stands; 18th-century Greek icon.

2. "The Golden Calf" (Ex. 32:1–8); copperplate engraving by H. Robinson, London, 18th century, after a painting by Nicholas Poussin.

3. Model by Moshe Levine of the Tabernacle, the portable sanctuary used in the wilderness (Ex. 25 ff.). In the court may be seen the bronze altar with its ramp, and behind it the sanctuary, which housed the Tables of the Law.

4. Archaeological shaft in the fortifications of Jericho, the first Canaanite city conquered by the Israelites (Josh. 6).

5. The Holy of Holies of an Israelite sanctuary uncovered at Arad, and dating from the tenth-ninth centuries B.C.E., the period of the early monarchy. It has been reconstructed in the Israel Museum, Jerusalem.

6. "Samson and Delilah" (Judg. 16); Van Dyck (1599–1661).

7. Valley of Elah, site of battle between David and Goliath (I Sam. 17), and where Israel's satellite station now stands.

THE JUDGES   SAUL   SOLOMON

DAVID

Philistines settle
in Erez Israel

Trojan Wars   I R O N   A G E

3
The Monarchy
Saul, David, Solomon (1150 B.C.E.—928 B.C.E.)

The threat of a mighty enemy forced the Israelites to hammer out their differences. During the 12th century B.C.E. the Philistines, sea raiders from Asia Minor, began to expand inland with speed and force. (Ultimately they gave the name Palestine to the country.) This danger could not be met piecemeal. The individual exploits of Samson (a figure of mighty strenght) merely slowed the tide. On other occasions, not even the presence of the Holy Ark amongst the Israelite soldiers prevented defeat. Only a king, capable of commanding the obedience of the whole people, could avert the danger. The prophet Samuel, the dominant personality of the period, did not initially agree with this policy. Eventually, however, he succumbed to popular pressure. Saul (c. 1020-04 B.C.E.) was anointed the first king of Israel. But Saul proved to be an unfortunate choice. His guerrilla campaign did free much of the country from the Philistine yoke, but he was ultimately deposed by Samuel for not exactly fulfilling God's command to destroy the Amalekites, an ancient foe.

His successor, whom Samuel anointed during Saul's lifetime, was a Judean farmer by the name of David. He had come into prominence when still a boy, by defeating a gigantic Philistine champion in single combat. Thereafter his daring exploits made him a popular choice. While Saul lived, however, David was forced to lead the life of an outlaw. Only his resourcefulness, and the devoted friendship of the king's son Jonathan, enabled him to survive. David was not safe until Saul (together with Jonathan) fell in battle against the Philistines on the slopes of Mount Gilboa.

There are few biblical characters whom we know more intimately than David. He is portrayed as a man of energy, genius and extremes. He was capable both of writing the most sublime lyric verse (traditionally the authorship of the Book of Psalms is attributed to him) and of committing some shameless wrongdoings. Yet it is not only for his personal characteristics that David is remembered. His importance lies in the political

benefits of his long reign. Firstly, he completed the unification of the nation. Having skillfully neutralized the rival claims of Saul's surviving son, he also won the somewhat tardy allegiance of the northern tribes. He then undertook a major reform of the national administration, and thereby converted the loose federation of clans into a strongly centralized kingdom. David's second achievement was the attainment of international renown. Under his leadership the Israelites swept the Philistines from the country and conducted a series of successful campaigns against other neighbors. By the time of his death, David's authority was recognized from the Egyptian border in the south, to the banks of the Euphrates in the north. Finally, David gave the Irsaelites what was to become their most cherished city. Quick to appreciate the strategic and commercial importance of Jerusalem (a city which he had himself conquered), he transformed it into Israel's capital, siting there both the Ark and the court. It is from the reign of David that the Jewish attachment to Jerusalem dates.

David's son and successor, Solomon (965-928 B.C.E.) consolidated his father's achievements. The Bible attributes the success with which he did so to his profound belief and his archetypal wisdom (he is traditionally regarded as the author of the Book of Proverbs). Solomon's reign was predominantly peaceful. David's empire was defended and enriched by his son's statecraft and diplomacy, not warfare. More than anyone before him did Solomon exploit the commercial potential of Palestine as the highway between Africa and Asia. His own merchant fleet ventured to Ophir, Tyre, and possibly Africa. Solomon also strengthened the administrative ties within the country, dividing it into 12 efficient units each subordinate to the capital. The climax of his reign came with the erection in the capital of a magnificent Temple, to house the national shrine. Jerusalem thus also became the religious center of the country, and the destination of pilgrims three times every year.

Motif: David and Goliath; miniature from the *British Museum Miscellany,* a French manuscript, c. 1280. "And he took his staff in his hand, and chose him five smooth stones out of the brook, and put them in the shepherd's bag which he had, . . . and his sling was in his hand; and he drew near to the Philistine" (I Samuel 17:40).

1. "The Visit of the Queen of Sheba to Solomon" (I Kings 10); detail from the painting by Jacopo Tintoretto (1518–94).

2. Samuel anoints David; a panel at Dura-Europos. "Then Samuel took the horn of oil, and anointed him in the midst of his brethren" (I Samuel 16:13).

3. "Saul and David"; an oil by Rembrandt, c. 1655. "And it came to pass, when the evil spirit from God was upon Saul, that David took the harp, and played with his hand; so Saul found relief, and it was well with him, and the evil spirit departed from him" (I Samuel 16:23).

4. This statue of David by Verrocchio, 1476, stands in Florence.

5. Aerial view of the Old City of Jerusalem. The shaded portion indicates the ancient City of David (early tenth century B.C.E.).

6. Map showing the extent of Solomon's kingdom (mid-tenth century B.C.E.).

7. "The Judgment of Solomon"; an oil by Rubens, c. 1615. "It shall be neither mine nor thine; divide it" (I Kings 3:16–28).

| SOLOMON | KINGDOM OF JUDAH | | | | | |
| KINGDOM OF ISRAEL | | | | | | |

| B.C.E. | 900 | 800 | 700 | 612 | 600 | 500 |

A R A M   D A M A S C U S   ASSYRIA   BABYLONIA

HOMER   Rome founded   SENNACHERIB   NEBUCHADNEZZAR

Fall of Nineveh

20

Division and Destruction
Judah and Israel (928 B.C.E.—587/6 B.C.E.)

Even during Solomon's lifetime dissension had again appeared. The king's numerous foreign wives imported pagan ideas, and his heavy taxation imposed intolerable burdens. At his death, David's magnificent empire fell apart. Solomon's son Rehoboam (928-911 B.C.E.) lost the affection of the people and the northern tribes proclaimed Jeroboam (928–907 B.C.E.) king of a separate state. For the next two centuries Israelites were divided into two neighboring and often warring kingdoms. The southern (Judah) retained the capital of Jerusalem, the northern (Israel) centered about Shechem. The schism was accentuated by the establishment within Israel of two new cultic centers, independent of Jerusalem.

Of the two kingdoms, the northern was the less stable. In only a minority of cases was a ruler of Israel succeeded by his own son; many met untimely and violent deaths. This contrasted with the situation in Judah, where the house of David never lacked an heir to occupy the throne of the great ancestor, and where the royal dynasty consequently acquired a far greater hold on popular sentiment. Yet for a brief period the northern kingdom appeared the more glorious. Judah was not only far smaller than Israel (of which it was often a dependency): it was also more isolated. The part which Judah played in international affairs for most of its existence was negligible. It commanded too few resources to either trouble, or be troubled by, the world outside. Israel's situation was completely different. Its geographical location, and the ambition of its rulers, propelled it to the mainstream of international life. Under such ruthless kings as Omri (882–71) and Ahab (871–52), Israel forged alliances with its neighbors, adopted some of their religious practices, and attracted great wealth into the country. Thus it was Omri who built the state's new capital city (Samaria) and Ahab who expanded it.

But success has its price. Popular discontent was aroused by brutal taxation and by the enforced worship of Baal, and such prophets as Elijah and Amos thundered against both. Foreign envy was aroused by the wealth of the country. Egypt in the south and Assyria in the north fostered both palace intrigues from within and hostile coalition from without. Caught between these giants, the rulers of Israel first prevaricated and then fell. In approximately 720 B.C.E. the kingdom of Israel was conquered by the Assyrians and the country populated by foreign settlers. The native inhabitants were exiled and lost all independence as well as identity. Legends concerning the "Ten Lost Tribes" and their fate continued to exist, but were unsubstantiated.

Any feeling of exultation which the kingdom of Judah might have felt at the fall of its sister state was qualified by the fact that the southern kingdom itself was now directly faced with Assyrian power. Year after year the Assyrian armies swept down upon Judah "like a wolf on the fold," and devastated the country. Admittedly Judah was not conquered by Assyria. On one occasion, Jerusalem was miraculously saved by a panic within the Assyrian camp, on another its defenses were assured by Hezekiah's famous provision of a new water supply. Moreover the Assyrian empire itself collapsed, and was replaced by the new colossus of Babylonia.

But the respite was temporary. Foreign influences had penetrated the southern kingdom too, and with them came idol worship. Only such a strong king as Josiah (639-09 B.C.E.) could combine a degree of political independence with the restoration of religious purity. Otherwise, however, the politics as well as the beliefs of the kings of Judah became the object of the criticism of such prophets as Isaiah and Jeremiah who advocated neutrality in external affairs no less than monotheism in religious thought.

The last attempts of the kings of Judah to obtain some form of independence by an Egyptian alliance (the mirage which had earlier proved fatal to Israel) were unavailing. In the winter of 588-587 Nebuchadnezzar, king of Babylon, laid siege to Jerusalem. In seven months he conquered the city, and on the ninth of Av his armies destroyed the Temple. Judah was laid waste. Most of the people were led captive to Babylon. After the murder of the local Jewish governor the remaining few inhabitants fled to Egypt. The first Jewish commonwealth had ended.

Post dies aut. siccat' ē torrens. Ilo enī plue
rat sup īram.

helias.

corui.

ficus de couruent.

act' ē q̄ sermo dn̄i ad eū dicens.

Motif: Winged sphinx in Phoenician style from the ninth-century Ivory Palace of Ahab in Samaria (I Kings 22:39).

1. The prophet Isaiah; detail from Michelangelo's ceiling in the Sistine Chapel.

2. Rehoboam speaks harshly to his subjects (I Kings 12:6–14); drawing by Hans Holbein, 1530.

3. Jeroboam sets golden calves in Beth El and Dan (I Kings 12:26–33); from the *Amiens Picture Bible*, Spain, 1197.

4. The prophet Elijah being fed by the ravens (I Kings 17:6); *Leon Bible*, Spain, 1162.

5. Panel from ninth-century B.C.E. Black Obelisk of Shalmaneser III, king of Assyria, showing Jehu, king of Israel, prostrating himself in surrender.

6. Siloam tunnel hewn by Hezekiah to bring water to embattled Jerusalem, c. 700 C.E. (II Kings 20:20).

7. The Wailing Wall, c. 1920. This retaining wall of the Temple Mount was built by Herod on the foundations of the ruins of the First Temple.

8. Nebuchadnezzar's army attacks the Temple in Jerusalem (587 B.C.E.; II Kings 25); a 15th-century French miniature by Jean Fouquet.

		Jerusalem destroyed			Cyrus' Edict	Temple			Second return				Events of
JUDAH					First return	rebuilt			under Ezra	NEHEMIAH			Purim
B.C.E.		600	586		538	525		500	458	450			400
		Babylonia conquered by Cyrus											SOCRATES
PERSIA													
			CYRUS								DARIUS II		
		Egypt conquered by Cambyses				CONFUCIUS						PELOPONNESIAN WARS	
				BUDDHA									

24

5

By the Waters of Babylon
The Exile (586 B.C.E.—444 B.C.E.)

The destruction of the state and Temple were traumatic experiences for the Judeans. Nevertheless the southern exiles (unlike the northern victims) managed to preserve their distinctive culture and their national consciousness. Such prophets as Isaiah and Jeremiah (who lived to lament the fall of Jerusalem) had predicted the catastrophe long before it occurred; they had also taught that the loss of independence was a divine punishment which might be both atoned for and avenged. Even in exile there arose eloquent teachers like Ezekiel, whose vivid orations exhorted the people to preserve their confidence and their faith.

Judaism was affected by the exile. With the Temple in Jerusalem in ruins, the synagogue, perhaps the most important institution in Jewish life, now became the center of religious activity. There, worship took the place of sacrifice, and prayer meetings, at which the ancient literature was expounded, now probably became regular institutions. The enforced juxtaposition of Jew and non-Jew also affected the former's theology, especially as contact between the two groups was often cordial. The exiles quickly accommodated themselves to their new conditions and enjoyed both prosperity and a degree of autonomy.

Thus for the first time, life in the Diaspora became thinkable. The Jewish communities of Babylon continued to flourish until the 10th century C.E.; other exilic centers, although shorter-lived, were equally significant. In Elephantine, an island in the Nile delta, some Jews constructed a temple in the service of God (It was destroyed by antagonistic priests in 411 B.C.E.). In Persia, a threatened decree of extinction was averted by royal influence. The festival of Purim, instituted to commemorate that deliverance, is to this day celebrated by the public reading of the Scroll of Esther and by various family and synagogue festivities.

But Judah remained the center of the people's hopes. From that country they even took their national name (*Yehudim*). When the Persians conquered Babylon and Cyrus, the new ruler, gave the Jews permission to return to Jerusalem and rebuild the Temple, they considered it a divine act. In 538 B.C.E. about 50,000 souls returned to the small area around Jerusalem assigned to them. Within a year they had reinstituted the sacrificial service. The accompanying jubilation proved premature. The work of restoration was delayed by both the demanding natural hazards and the debilitating opposition of the neighboring tribes. The colonists whom the Assyrians had settled in the northern kingdom proved particularly troublesome. Known as Samaritans, the members of this group had themselves accepted a form of Judaism (which their descendants practice today) and were preparing to build their own temple on Mount Gerizim. By means fair and foul this rival element systematically obstructed the work of reconstruction. Ezra, who had led a further 180,000 Babylonian Jews to Palestine in 458 B.C.E., was appointed governor of Judah and attempted to rebuild the walls of Jerusalem. Even he, however, had to desist after Samaritan complaints. That particular task was not completed until 445 B.C.E. when Nehemiah, an influential Babylonian Jew, was himself appointed governor. It was also Nehemiah who, in a solemn ceremony of dedication, impressed on the people the importance of defending their walls, appointing guards for the city and constructing a citadel there. With at least one fortified stronghold, the Jewish settlers in Palestine had thus constructed the nucleus of a state.

Ezra and Nehemiah joined forces in 445 B.C.E. Under their joint guidance the work of moral regeneration accompanied that of political reconstruction. Ezra read the Torah at a convocation of the entire people, who later solemnly undertook to live in accordance with its laws. Nehemiah, after an absence during which a reaction had apparently set in, instituted various other religious measures as a result of which the schism with the Samaritans became final. The era of the two leaders thus became the first period of the reign of the Torah. The rule of the teacher (rabbi) superseded even that of the priest, and the laxity of the original returnees was replaced by the faith of their descendants. The practices which initially had to be enforced were now adopted with ungrudging zeal.

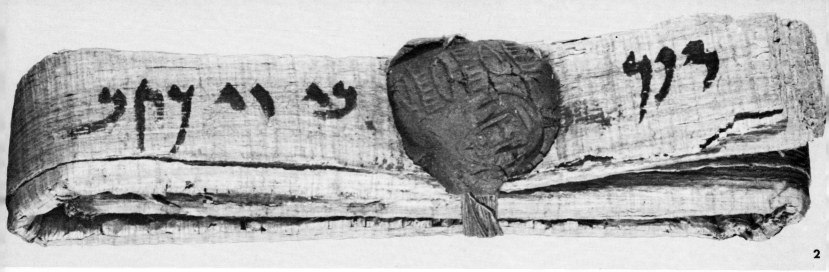

2

3

4

5

Motif: Darius, king of Persia (442–404 B.C.E.), sketched from rock relief at Bisutun, Iran.

1. Ezekiel's vision of the valley of dry bones (ch. 37); a panel from the Knesset *menorah* by Benno Elkan.

2. Aramaic papyrus scroll from the Jewish community of Elephantine, fifth century B.C.E.

3. Scenes from the Purim story; mural from Dura-Europos synagogue.

4. Parchment *megillah* or Esther Scroll, illuminated by Shalom Italia, c. 1673; roller has ivory figurines of Esther and Ahasuerus.

5. Tomb of Cyrus, king of Persia (559–529 B.C.E.), at Pasargadae, Iran.

6. Ezra teaches the Law to the contrite people (chs. 9–10); a panel from the Knesset *menorah* by Benno Elkan.

7. Nehemiah depicted in an Armenian manuscript Bible, c. 1653.

8. Descendants of the ancient Samaritans still sacrifice the paschal lamb on Mt. Gerizim.

27

Alexander conquers
Erez Israel

Ptolemy I conquers
Erez Israel

B.C.E. 350		332		300		250

SELEUCID DYNASTY IN SYRIA

ALEXANDER THE GREAT   PTOLEMAIC DYNASTY IN EGYPT

ROME   1st Punic War

6

The Bible
Its Impact and Language

Thus far, our account of the Hebrew race has followed the traditional treatment embodied in the Old Testament (whose narrative ends with Nehemiah). Any attempt to do otherwise is unjustifiable. No other source matches either the style of the biblical narrative, nor its corporate body of national tradition. Scholars differ as to the authenticity and dating of various biblical episodes, but none deny either the importance or beauty of the work.

Jewish tradition divides the books of the Bible into three sections. Together these are known as the *Tanakh*, from the initial letters of the Hebrew names of each section.

The first, known as the Torah, relates the story of the Creation of the world and the early history of the Hebrews from the time of the patriarchs until the entry into the Land of Canaan. This section also comprises the code of law which has subsequently become the basis for all Jewish religious and legal practice. According to tradition, these books were written by Moses at God's dictation.

The second section of the Bible is known as Nevi'im (Prophets). Its early books consist of historical records which relate fortunes of the people during the seven centuries following the entry into Canaan, until the destruction of the First Temple. Later books in this section contain records of the utterances of various prophets who constituted the watchdogs of the national conscience throughout the period of the two kingdoms. Occasionally it has proved difficult to provide exact dates for certain of the shorter (minor) prophetic books.

The third section of the Bible, Ketuvim (Writings or Hagiographa) is a composite miscellany, containing an anthology of historical, devotional, dramatic and poetic literature.

The Bible does not contain all the Jewish literature to have survived from the pre-Christian era. The canon was chosen by the rabbis from a great variety of works, some of which still exist in the Apocrypha (i.e., the external books). The rabbis did not finalize the canon until the mishnaic period (first century C.E.) and the traditional texts were not established until seven or eight centuries later. Thereafter the accepted format was not changed. Even the Isaiah scroll discovered in the Qumran caves (of no later date than the first century C.E.) reveals only slight variations from the accepted version. By the tenth century the pointing and cantillation had been fixed.

Ultimately it is the Bible which makes the study of early Jewish history different from that of numerous other contemporary nations. Denied acquaintance with the civilized code of early Hebrew law, or of the supreme call of the prophets, mankind would be not only more ignorant but also poorer in spirit. For this reason the Old Testament has been accepted as the authentic word of God by Christians and Moslems, as well as Jews. For the latter it is the Book of Books. The study of its text is a religious duty to which thousands of commentaries bear witness. In the synagogue, regular public readings of the Torah, supplemented by texts from the prophets, have occupied a central place in the service for well over 2,000 years.

The language of the Bible has proved of hardly less consequence than its content. It has been translated into the vast majority of the world's languages, and in many instances has greatly influenced native linguistic styles. Its greatest linguistic contribution of all has been to Hebrew. Since biblical times the appearance of the Hebrew characters has undergone several changes, as has their pronunciation. Yet despite these changes Hebrew, because it was the language of the Bible, has remained both the holy and the national tongue. Even when Hebrew ceased to be a spoken language (after c. 70 C.E.) and was replaced by either Aramaic, the vernacular, or various Jewish dialects, the language and style of the Bible continued to be copied and used in prayer, study, and correspondence. It was on this basis that, guided by the efforts of such men as Eliezer Ben Yehuda (1857-1922), the modern State of Israel was able to revive Hebrew as the national language.

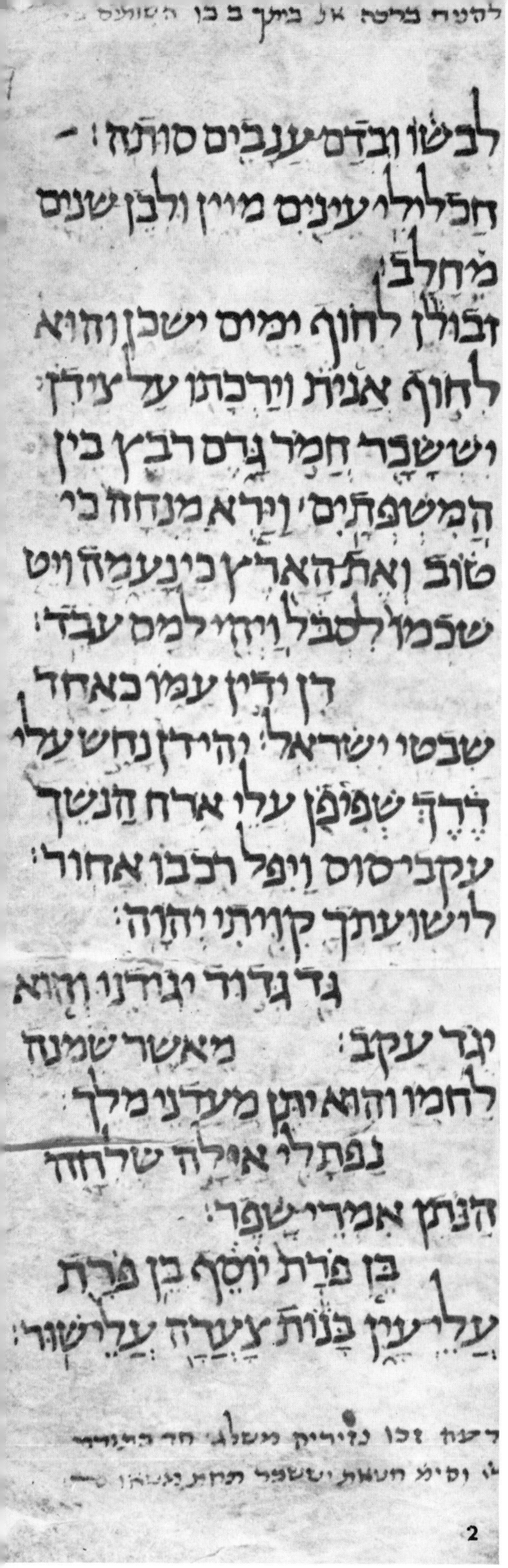

לחמה ברכה אל ביתך ב בו השולם

לבשו ובדם־ענבים סותה ׀ -
חכלילי עינים מיין ולבן שנים
מחלב׃
זבולן לחוף ימים ישכן והוא
לחוף אנית וירכתו על־צידן
יששכר חמר גרם רבץ בין
המשפתים׃ וירא מנחה כי
טוב ואת־הארץ כי נעמה ויט
שכמו לסבל ויהי למס עבד׃
דן ידין עמו כאחד
שבטי ישראל׃ יהי־דן נחש עלי־
דרך שפיפן עלי־ארח הנשך
עקבי־סוס ויפל רכבו אחור׃
לישועתך קויתי יהוה׃
גד גדוד יגודנו והוא
יגד עקב׃   מאשר שמנה
לחמו והוא יתן מעדני־מלך׃
נפתלי אילה שלחה
הנתן אמרי־שפר׃
בן פרת יוסף בן פרת
עלי־עין בנות צעדה עלי־שור׃

דעת זכו נזיריק משלגי חד כיגודיר
ני וסיל חעאת ישפר תחת נעית ....

2

30

לרכה זה התל
פה ויצו זוה
כרד והוה
וילה הפתח

3

4

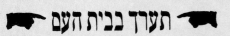

אספת מחאה

נגד יחס הועד המפקח
של הטכניקום בחיפה
אל השפה העברית

תערך בבית העם

היום י' חשון, בשעה שמונה בערב.

באספה ישתתפו: בית־העם, ועד הלשון, אגרת המורים, תסתדרת העברית, אגרת
הרופאים העברים בירושלים, בצלאל, הסתדרת הקרמונים הבבכר, פועלי
ציון, הפועל־הצעיר, ועדת הברית, האגרה העולמת של החפאר הערבת

חתר הסכנ

ועד בית העם

5

6

7

מה ענו אהלי־עק

8

9

31

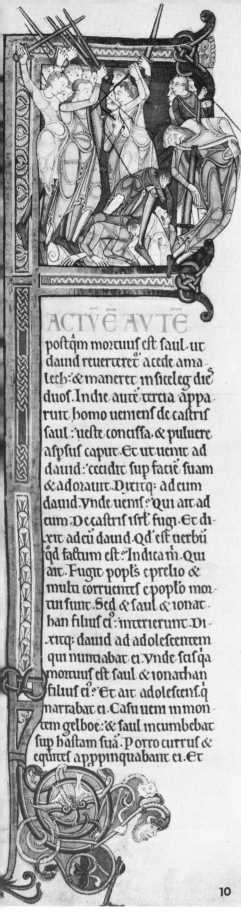

ACTVM AVTE

postqm mortuus est saul. ut
dauid reuerteret a cede ama-
lech: & maneret in sicelet die
duos. In die aut tertia appa-
ruit homo ueniens de castris
saul: ueste conscissa. & puluere
aspsus caput. Et ut uenit ad
dauid: cecidit sup facie suam
& adorauit. Dixitq; ad eum
dauid. Vnde uenis? Qui ait ad
eum. De castris isrl fugi. Et di-
xit ad eu dauid. Qd est uerbu
qd factum est: Indica m. Qui
ait. Fugit popls e prelio: &
multi corruentes e poplo mor-
tui sunt. Sed & saul & ionathan filius ei: interierunt. Dixitq; dauid ad adolescentem
qui nuntiabat ei. Vnde scis qa
mortuus est saul & ionathan
filius ei? Et ait adolescens.q
narrabat ei. Casu ueni in mon-
tem gelboe: & saul incumbebat
sup hastam sua. Porro currus &
equites appppinquabant ei. Et

10

32

ΚΑΙΕΠΛΥΝΑΝΤΑΪΜΑΤΙΑ
ΚΑΙΕΙΠΕΝΤΩΛΑΩΓΙΝΕϹ
ΘΕΕΤ.ΟΙΜΟΙΤΡΕΙϹΗΜΕΡΑϹ
ΜΗΠΡΟϹΕΛΘΗΤΕΓΥΝΑΙΚΙ
ΕΓΕΝΕΤΟΔΕΤΗΗΜΕΡΑΤΗ
ΤΡΙΤΗΓΕΝΗΘΕΝΤΟϹΠΡ
ΟΡΘΡΟΝΚΑΙΕΓΙΝΟΝΤΟ
ΦΩΝΑΙΚΑΙΑϹΤΡΑΠΑΙ·
ΚΑΙΝΕΦΕΛΗΓΝΟΦΩΔ
ΕΠΟΡΟΥϹϹΕΙΝΑΦΩΝΗ
ΤΗϹϹΑΛΠΙΓΓΟϹΗΧΕΙΜΕ
ΓΑΚΑΙΕΠΤΟΗΘΗΠΑϹΟ
ΛΑΟϹΟΕΝΤΗΠΑΡΕΜΒΟ
ΛΗ ΚΑΙΕΞΗΓΑΓΕΝΜΩΥ
ϹΗϹΤΟΝΛΑΟΝΕΙϹϹΥΝΑ
ΤΗϹΙΝΤΟΥΘΥΕΚΤΗϹΠΑ
ΡΕΜΒΟΛΗϹΚΑΙΠΑΡΕϹΤΗ
ϹΑΝΥΠΟΤΟΟΡΟϹϹΙΝΑ
ΤΟΔΕΟΡΟϹΤΟϹΙΝΑΕΚΑ·
ΠΝΙΖΕΤΟΟΛΟΝΔΙΑΤΟ
ΚΑΤΑΒΕΒΗΚΕΝΑΙΕΠΑΥ
ΤΟΤΟΝΘΝΕΝΠΥΡΙΚΑΙ
ΑΝΕΒΑΙΝΕΝΟΚΑΠΝΟϹ
ωϹΚΑΠΝΟϹΚΑΜΕΙΝΟΥ
ΚΑΙΕΞΕϹΤΗΠΑϹΟΛΑΟϹ
ϹΦΟΔΡΑ ΕΓΙΝΟΝΤΟΔΕ
ΑΙΦΩΝΑΙΤΗϹϹΑΛΠΙΓΓΟϹ
ΠΡΟΒΑΙΝΟΥϹΑΪϹΧΥΡΟ
ΤΕΡΑΙϹΦΟΔΡΑΜΩϹΗϹ·
ΕΛΑΛΗϹΕΝΟΔΕΘϹΑΠΕ·
ΚΡΕΙΝΑΤΟΑΥΤΩΦΩΝΗ
ΚΑΤΕΒΗΔΕΚϹΕΠΙΤΟΟΡ
ΤΟϹΙΝΑΕΠΙΤΗΝΚΟΡΥΦ
ΤΟΥΟΡΟΥϹΚΑΙΕΚΑΛΕϹΕ
ΚϹΜΩΥϹΗΝΕΠΙΤΗΝΚΟ
ΡΥΦΗΝΤΟΥΟΡΟΥϹΚΑΙΑ
ΝΕΒΗΜΩΥϹΗϹ
ΚΑΙΕΙΠΕΝΟΘϹΠΡΟϹΜΩΥ
ϹΗΝΛΕΓΩΝ ΚΑΤΑΒΑϹΔΙ
ΑΜΑΡΤΥΡΑΙΤΩΛΑΩΜΗ·
ΠΟΤΕΕΓΓΙϹΩϹΙΝΠΡΟϹ
ΤΟΝΘΝΚΑΤΑΝΟΗϹΑΙΚΑΙ
ΠΕϹωϹΙΝΕΞΑΥΤΩΝΠΛΗ
ΘΟϹΚΑΙΟΙΪΕΡΕΙϹΟΙΕΓΓΙ

11

Juif de Caïfum lisant la Bible à la
chaire de Moyse, avec deux souffleurs 12

13

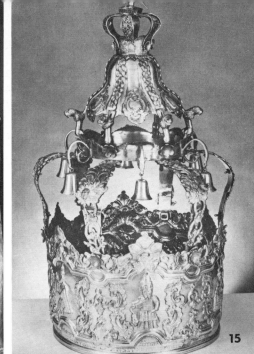

Motif: Hebrew cursive script of the sixth-fifth centuries B.C.E. on an incantation bowl from Babylonia.

1. The opening of one of the Dead Sea Scrolls, which include biblical manuscripts dating from the last two centuries of the Second Temple.

2. Hebrew square script in Egyptian manuscript of Genesis, c. tenth century C.E.

3. "Hither were brought the bones of Uzziah, King of Judah. Do not open." Hebrew inscription, end of Second Temple period.

4. With bamboo pen and parchment scroll, this Yemenite Torah scribe writes the 15th chapter of Genesis.

5. Eliezer Ben-Yehuda, Hebrew lexicographer, in 1910.

6. Poster of protest meeting against the Haifa Technion's decision (1913) to use German as its official language of instruction.

7. Pentateuch with commentaries, printed on parchment in Spain, 1490.

8. Session of the Fourth International Bible Contest in Jerusalem.

9. Latin Bible, France, 12th century; illuminated initial letter 'H' depicts Moses speaking to the Children of Israel.

10. *Lambeth Bible*, England, 12th century; illumination of "Death of Saul and his Sons" (I Samuel 31:1–6).

11. Exodus manuscript of the Septuagint, fifth century.

12. Reading the Torah in the Kaifeng synagogue; drawing by a Jesuit missionary, 18th century.

13. Torah scroll in Sephardi-style case from India.

14. Wrapper for Torah scroll, Germany, 1813; embroidered text includes a child's name, birthday, and appropriate zodiac sign.

15. Silver crown for Torah scroll; Germany, 18th century.

16. Holy Ark, repository of the Torah scrolls; Landesbilstelle synagogue, Berlin, before *Kristallnacht*, 1938.

Judah Maccabee
conquers Jerusalem

Hasmonean revolt

H A S M O N E A N S

B.C.E.

200

167

164

100

SYRIA

ANTIOCHUS IV EPIPHANES

3rd Punic War

ROME

7
The Maccabees
The Struggle Against Hellenism (444 B.C.E.—164 B.C.E.)

Although little is known of the internal history of the Jews after Nehemiah's death, the fourth and third centuries B.C.E. were formative periods in the nation's religious life. The process known as the interpretation of the Torah then began. New laws relevant to contemporary conditions, together with moral and ethical axioms, were gradually inferred from the original biblical text. The religious patterns that consequently emerged remained the basis of Jewish life. National sentiment also crystallized around religious personages. A Great Synod of sages (*ha-Knesset ha-Gedolah*) interpreted the Torah, and the High Priest exercised a secular as well as a sacerdotal role. One High Priest, Simon the Just, was later regarded as the ideal religious leader.

Changes in the international scene caused more immediate transformations. Late in the fourth century, the Persian empire collapsed before the onslaught of Alexander of Macedon, and the Jews, together with their neighbors, came under his rule. This event was decisive; for the next ten centuries Judah was dominated by rulers deriving their main source of inspiration from Greece or Rome, not the Orient. Initially the Jews remained largely autonomous, subject only to annual tributes, and their internal religious life was hardly affected. But the struggle waged by Alexander's successors again transformed Judah into a buffer territory between Egypt (under Ptolemy) and Syria (under Seleucus). Although the country passed definitely under Seleucid rule in 198 B.C.E., by then a new power, Rome, had begun to challenge Syrian hegemony in the Middle East. Believing that uniformity was the best guarantee of unity, the Seleucids determined to transform Judah completely into a Syrian province.

Antiochus IV, who ruled Syria from 174 to 164 B.C.E., decided to achieve this objective by uprooting Jewish particularist religious customs, and replacing them with Hellenistic culture. Some Jewish aristocrats had anticipated his policy; they had already begun to imitate the Greek language and manners of their masters, and to temporize even in religious matters. Thus,

they built a gymnasium in Jerusalem, designed to supersede the Temple, and substituted the worship of the human body for that of God. But the process of Hellenization was proceeding too slowly for Antiochus and he initiated more forceful measures to eradicate Judaism. The observance of the Sabbath and of circumcision became capital crimes; the worship of deities and the consumption of such forbidden food as swine were enforced by arms. The Temple was desecrated, and renamed for the Olympian Zeus. Not even the hereditary high priesthood was immune to this interference and Menelaus, who was not even of priestly descent, was appointed.

Much to the chagrin of Antiochus, most Jews refused to share his admiration for Greek culture, preferring to suffer martyrdom for their faith. One group, the Ḥasidim (pietists), fostered a messianic belief that the unprecedented suffering would soon be followed by the downfall of evil and fulfillment of the promised End of Days. Ultimately the Jews rose in revolt. In 167 B.C.E. Mattathias, a priest of the Hasmonean family, cut down a co-religionist preparing to sacrifice at the pagan altar erected in his local village of Modi'in. Then, together with his five sons, Mattathias escaped into the hills and raised the standard of rebellion.

There followed a classic case of successful guerrilla warfare. The Hasmoneans enjoyed the advantages of undaunted faith, local sympathy, and knowledge of the terrain. Their movement was also peculiarly fortunate in its leaders. Few families in history can boast of the military gallantry and political ability displayed by the Hasmonean brothers. They exploited both the immobility of the large Syrian armies and the domestic difficulties of the Seleucid dynasty. Under the leadership of the third son, Judah "the Maccabee," they finally won their liberty of worship. On the 25th Kislev, 164 B.C.E., the Temple was liberated, purified and rededicated. In remembrance of that event the festival of Hanukkah has been celebrated ever since, with candles being lit for eight successive days.

2

3

4

5

Motif: Seleucid combat squad advances to crush Hasmonean revolt (I Macc. 6: 30); from a Low German Bible, Cologne, 1478–80.

1. Alexander the Great paying homage to the High Priest; 13th-century illuminated Latin Bible.

2. Greek motifs decorate this limestone ossuary of the Second Temple period, found near Jerusalem.

3. Hellenistic remains at Ashkelon from c. 100 B.C.E.; a relief of Nike, the Greek goddess of victory, standing on the globe supported by Atlas.

4. Painted tomb of the third-second centuries B.C.E. at Mareshah, Erez Israel, typical of the Hellenistic tombs found throughout the Middle East.

5. Marble tablet from Delos in the Aegean Sea, inscribed in Greek with a prayer asking for vengeance for the murder of two Jewish women in the second century B.C.E., the period of Seleucid oppression.

6. Remains of a temple erected over a cave at Banias in the Golan Heights, in honor of the Greek god Pan.

7. Judah Maccabee; enamel plaque, France, 16th century.

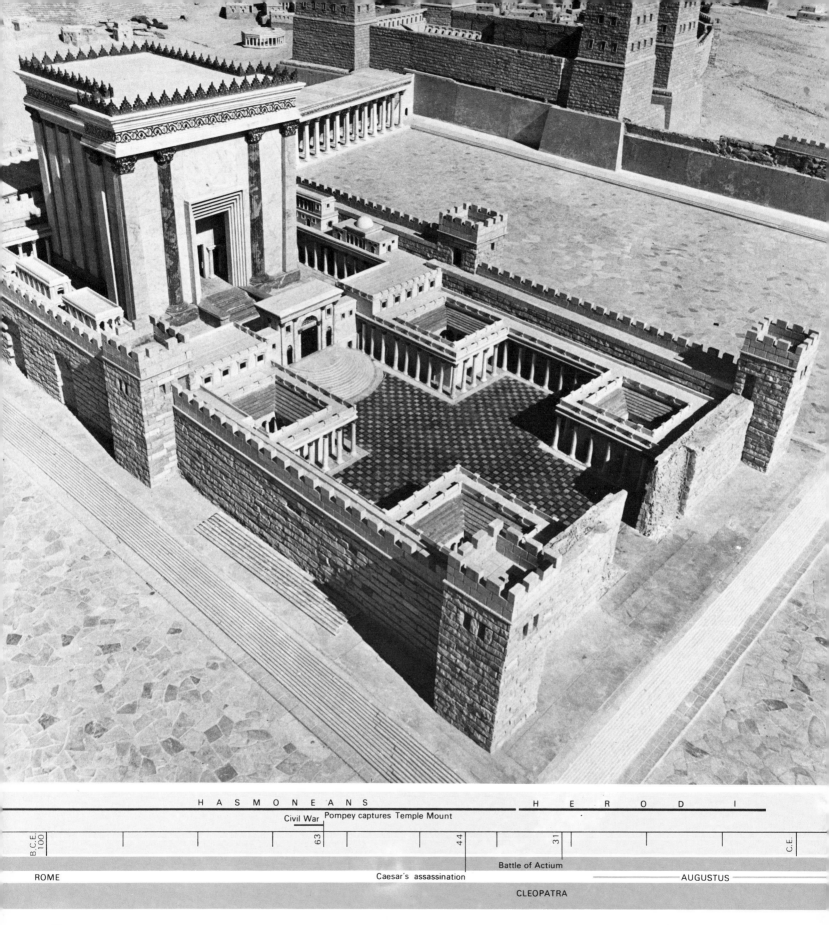

H A S M O N E A N S   H E R O D I

Civil War   Pompey captures Temple Mount

B.C.E. 100   63   44   31   C.E.

Battle of Actium

ROME   Caesar's assassination   AUGUSTUS

CLEOPATRA

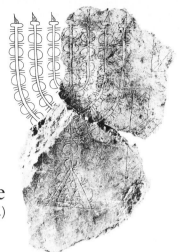

8

The Hasmonean State
Independence (164 B.C.E.—63 B.C.E.)

Having won their religious freedom, the Hasmoneans enlarged the aims of their revolt. For the first time since the Exile a movement for political independence developed. Although Judah was killed in battle and Jonathan (the fourth brother) was treacherously murdered, the Jews continued to exploit the internal decay of Syria. Led by Simeon (the fifth son), they finally won their independence in 142 B.C.E. Two years later Simeon was proclaimed ethnarch (civil ruler), High Priest, and commander-in-chief of the army. His successors assumed royal prerogatives. The Hasmonean kingdom had been founded.

Simeon's son, John Hyrcanus, inherited an enlarged state. Both Jonathan and Simeon had undertaken successful expeditions against their neighbors. Hyrcanus further expanded Judah's borders. Like his predecessors, he carefully maintained friendly relations with the advancing, although still distant, power of Rome. He also led expeditions into Transjordan and began to expand northwards. Finally he annexed the neighboring state of Idumea (Edom), converting its whole population to Judaism. Hyrcanus' son completed his conquests. Aristobulus conquered the Galilee; Alexander Yannai expanded into Transjordan. A century after Mattathias' revolt, the Hasmonean state thus rivalled in extent the size of David's glorious empire.

Simultaneously, Jewish settlement outside Palestine increased in strength. Egypt housed a particularly large Jewish population, famed for its learning no less than its wealth. During this period the scholars of Alexandria translated the Bible into Greek (the Septuagint) and developed their own cultural tradition. This process culminated with Philo (20 B.C.E.-45 C.E.), who attempted to combine the best of Jewish and Hellenistic cultures.

Within Judah itself, external expansion was not accompanied by internal cohesion. The massive tide of enthusiasm which had contributed to initial Hasmonean successes had begun to wane before Hyrcanus' death. The dynasty continued to enjoy the support of the powerful priestly elect, but other sectors of the people objected to the conjunction in one person of the authority of both high priest and king—especially since royalty was traditionally restricted to the House of David. Ultimately two parties developed in the state: one recruited from the priestly aristocracy, the other from the lower and middle classes. Their conflict was intensified by differences in religious outlook. The priestly party, called Sadducees (probably after a biblical high priest Zadok) represented the religious establishment, insisting on the exclusive centrality of the Temple and strict adherence to the letter of the written Law. Their opponents, the Pharisees (meaning separatists), were a more popular party. They stressed the importance of the house of learning, and denied that knowledge was the prerogative of the priesthood. They read more far-reaching meanings into the scriptural texts than did the Sadducees, and developed such new doctrines as the ressurrection of the body, and immortality of the soul, and the belief in angels. The Pharisees also concentrated on educational work amongst the people. In this they differed from other contemporary sects (amongst whom the Essenes were prominent) who were isolationist in outlook and practice.

The rift erupted violently during Yannai's reign. Acting like the passionate oriental despot he was, the king publicly insulted and then persecuted the Pharisees. His widow and successor, Salome Alexandra (who ruled 76-67 B.C.E.), effected a compromise, giving the Pharisees direction of the state under her brother, Simeon ben Shetaḥ. But her death renewed the civil war, with her two sons championing the rival parties. The victory of the younger, Aristobulus, was transitory. By 63 B.C.E. the power to decide the succession no longer lay with the Jews. Each side sought external support and the Roman legions led by Pompey decided the issue. The crown became a Roman political prize, not a distinguished Jewish inheritance. After a further series of civil wars, Mark Antony deposed the Maccabeans. Herod, an Idumean whose family had proved adroit politicians and skillful administrators, became king. In fact, though not yet in name, Judah had become a Roman province.

Motif: Plaster fragments of earliest known representation of Temple *menorah*, found in Old City of Jerusalem in 1969, and dating from reign of Herod, when the Temple still stood.

1. Herod's Temple as seen from east; model constructed on the blueprint of Prof. Michael Avi-Yonah.

2. Excavations at the Citadel in Old City show base of Herod's Phasael Tower (left) and Hasmonean fortifications.

3. Typical Herodian masonry; South Wall of the Temple Mount, with pilgrims' pavement leading up to the Temple gates.

4. Aerial view of Herod's fortified palace at Masada.

5. Aqueduct at Caesarea built by Herod, and restored by Roman legions at outbreak of Bar Kokhba Revolt.

6. The fortress of Herodium near Bethlehem.

7. Herodian amphitheater at Caesarea, with relics of superimposed fourth-century Byzantine fortress.

8. Jerusalem after the death of Herod; model in grounds of Holyland Hotel, Jerusalem.

Crucifixion
of Jesus

Destruction
of Jerusalem

Masada

Bar Kokhba

C.E.

30

70

100

132
135

200

Philo in
Alexandria

Death of
Paul of Tarsus

ROME

HADRIAN

MARCUS AURELIUS

9
The Roman Province
Judea Capta (63 B.C.E.—135 C.E.)

Herod's long reign displayed two contrasting facets. At one level he made serious attempts to win support among the Jews. In order to legitimize his rule he married Mariamne, a daughter of the Hasmonean house; in order to popularize it he was careful not to flaunt traditional religious laws and customs. He also brought the country an unusually protracted period of peace and apparent glory. His diplomatic skills enlarged the area under his sway, his commercial talent increased his wealth, and his passion for grandeur adorned it with such beautiful cities as Caesarea. Most notably, he undertook a lavish reconstruction of the Temple. This was acknowledged to be one of the wonders of the Mediterranean world.

But competence was not a recipe for adoration. Herod never won the hearts of the Jewish people nor of the sages, who always regarded him as a usurper and a tyrant. They never forgave him for murdering almost every member of his own family, the tragic victims of Herod's pathological suspicion of rival claimants to the throne. Neither did they share Herod's adoration of Hellenistic culture, against which the Maccabees had originally fought. Most obnoxious of all was the undeniable fact of Roman overlordship, on which depended Herod's every achievement. Roman legions encamped in Jerusalem, Roman institutions superseded the Sanhedrin of sages in government, and a Roman eagle dominated the entrance to the Temple. Although Herod himself managed ruthlessly to quell sporadic popular outbreaks during his lifetime, his death in 4 B.C.E. was succeeded by a general flare-up of insurrection. The Roman reaction was swift, brutal, and uncompromising. With the brief exception of Herod's grandson, Agrippa, the royal title fell into abeyance, and the facade of Jewish independence disappeared. The Jews were now directly ruled by a series of unsympathetic Roman procurators and subjected to exorbitantly heavy taxes.

Under the misgovernment of the procurators unrest became endemic. Bands of Zealots became especially active in the north, and Judah won notoriety as the most inflammable of all Roman provinces. In 30 C.E. the nervous administration even crucified a Galilean preacher named Jesus, most probably because he assumed the title King of the Jews. A concerted revolt broke out in 66 C.E., when the Temple authorities refused to offer the usual sacrifices for the welfare of the Roman people and rulers, and the Roman garrison in Jerusalem was butchered. A punitive force sent from Syria was defeated in the passes around Jerusalem and a provisional independent government established within the city. Throughout the country the Jews were called to arms. But even in this grave hour they lacked internal unity; Jewish energies were wasted on a struggle between extremist and moderate elements, and the rebels' strength was impaired by the defection of Josephus, a governor of the Galilee. Accordingly the Jewish resistance crumbled before the strong Roman army led by Vespasian. In the year 70 C.E. he besieged Jerusalem, leaving his son, Titus, to take the city. On the 9th of Av—the anniversary of the fall of the first Temple—Titus destroyed the Second Temple and carried its ornaments in triumph to Rome. Ever since, that day has been observed as a fast (Tish'ah be-Av). Only the remote fortress of Masada, situated on the Dead Sea and occupied by a small party of extremists, continued to resist. It was not overcome until its desperate defenders committed mass suicide in 73 C.E.

The tragedy had one further bloodthirsty sequel. Within a generation of the fall of Jerusalem the Jews, unable to accept their defeat, again rose in revolt. The first outburst of 115-117 C.E. was followed by another rising, provoked by the Emperor Hadrian's decision to establish a Roman city on the ruins of Jerusalem, in 132 C.E. Led by the fascinating figure of Bar Kokhba and supported by Rabbi Akiva, the greatest scholar of the generation, it enjoyed three years of unprecedented success. Jerusalem was liberated and commemorative coins were struck. But the military might of Rome proved invincible. In 134/5 C.E. the insurgents were slaughtered at Betar, Jerusalem itself was razed, and the practice of the Jewish religion outlawed.

5

7

6

8

9

10

11

12

13

Motif: Ostracon from the fortress of Masada inscribed "ben Ya'ir," possibly referring to Eleazar ben Ya'ir, Zealot commander at Masada, 73 C.E.

1. Stones hurled by the defenders of the Herodium fortress near Bethlehem, during the Bar Kokhba Revolt, 132–135 C.E.

2. Unopened scroll of the Thanksgiving Psalms, one of the many documentary relics of the Dead Sea sects of the late Second Temple period.

3. The interior of Jerusalem's Shrine of the Book, built in the grounds of the Israel Museum to house the Dead Sea Scrolls and related artifacts.

4. The excavated sectarian settlement at Qumran (lower right); the Scrolls, stored in large earthenware vessels, were found in caves in the nearby cliffs.

5. Woman carries the cross in the traditional Easter procession in Jerusalem.

6. Coin of 71 C.E.; obverse shows Vespasian, conqueror of Jerusalem, with laurel wreath, while reverse shows the figure of Judea, manacled and cowed, and encircled by the Latin inscription IUDAEA DEVICTA.

7. Lamenting the destruction of the Temple at the Wailing Wall, c. 1880.

8. *Mikveh* for ritual immersion, uncovered by Yiga'el Yadin at Masada. Its dimensions were found to conform precisely to the specifications of the *halakhah*.

9. Stone cups of the Zealot defenders of Masada.

10. Volunteer cleans Herodian mosaic floor in the Western Palace at Masada.

11. Women's artifacts from 135 C.E. found in the Cave of Letters in the Judean Desert; relics of the Bar Kokhba Revolt.

12. Coin of Bar Kokhba Revolt, dated in accordance with the rebels' shortlived calendar "Year One of the Redemption of Israel," i.e. 132 C.E.

13. Passage under Herodium fortress, used during the Bar Kokhba Revolt.

T A L M U D

Jews become
Roman citizens

Jews in Germany

| 200 | 212 | | | | 300 | | | | 400 | | | 500 |

CONSTANTINE I

ROME

End of Western Roman Empire

DIOCLETIAN

10

The Rule of the Rabbis
The Reorganization of Jewish Life

The fall of Jerusalem did not destroy either the Jewish religion or the Jewish people. Instead that upheaval, catastrophic though it was, led to vital developments in Jewish life. Some of these had already been anticipated during the first Exile. Now, as then, the longing for a messianic age of the future superseded the attempt to conserve the achievements of the present. Similarly, the local synagogues again had to take the place formerly occupied by the one central Temple. Once again, the high priesthood was divested of its essential functions, and the people looked elsewhere for religious guidance. In this latter sphere the period after the second destruction differed from its predecessor. Even after the year 70 C.E., the rabbis—scholars who expounded the Torah—had been revered and had become the recognized leaders of the Pharisee party. Despite their conflict with the authorities (both Hasmonean and Roman) their personal example and profound scholarship had already won them respect. Now, with the Sadducee party destroyed, they also assumed authority.

Just before Jerusalem fell, one outstanding Pharisee scholar, Johanan ben Zakkai, had contrived to escape from the city. The Romans permitted him to settle in the coastal town of Jabneh, and to open an academy there for the study of traditional lore. After the fall of Jerusalem, it was Jabneh which became the seat of the Sanhedrin (Supreme Court), a body which ultimately acquired semi-official political status. Its president (Nasi) became recognized as the representative of the Jewish people in its relations with the Roman authorities, and was left to reorganize Jewish life. Led for ten generations by the family of Rabban Gamaliel, the presidents successfully instituted a sub-government of their own, even after Hadrianic persecutions had moved the center of their activities to the Galilee. They maintained courts for deciding legal cases in accordance with Jewish law and houses of study for the exposition of the Torah. The change was one of substance as well as form. The scholar now became the dominating influence in Jewish affairs, and

erudition rather than wealth became the principal qualification for membership of the Sanhedrin. The group of rabbis around the Nasi thus established a personal ideal which was to retain its impact for many centuries to come.

Ultimately, the position and influence of the Nasi withered away. The remaining Jews in Judah suffered from the increasingly severe effects of agrarian devastation, exorbitant Roman taxation and, ultimately, Christian persecution. Even such monetary support as they received from the dispersed Jewish communities ceased once the Roman Empire was divided into its western and Byzantine sections. When in 425 Gamaliel VI died without male issue, the position of Nasi was abolished entirely. Long before then, however, the office had reached its apogee under Judah ha-Nasi, the most commanding personality of the period. It was he who edited the body of laws known as the Mishnah, and in so doing laid the basis for subsequent Jewish development. The importance of his work cannot be underestimated. Hitherto, the rabbis had relied on no written text other than the Bible. Legends, ethical teachings, and "case law" had of necessity evolved, and indeed were believed to consist of a tradition received by Moses at Sinai. But these teachings had been transmitted orally. The Hadrianic persecutions made it impossible to rely on this method any longer. Instead, Judah ha-Nasi revised and re-arranged the material at his disposal into six "Orders." Each order was written in pure Hebrew and treated a particular subject in a detail which the brevity of the Bible had precluded. The outlook which had previously led the Sadducees to accept none other than the literal interpretation of such Mosaic principles as "an eye for an eye" was finally overcome. Henceforth, it was to be the more exegetical Pharisean interpretation of monetary compensation (in that particular case) which proved dominant. Even set rules according to which the Scriptures should be understood were developed. Under these conditions, what emerged was a code of life which was to govern the actions of individual Jews for succeeding generations.

2

4

286

מאמתי קורין את שמע בערבית
משעה שהכהנים נכנסים לאכל
בתרומתן עד סוף האשמורה
הראשונה דברי ר' אליעזר וחכ' אומ'
עד חצות רבן גמליאל אומ' עד
שיעלה עמוד השחר ב
מעשה שבאו בניו מבית המשתה
אמרו לו לא קרינו את שמע אמר
להם אם לא עלה עמוד השחר
מותרין אתם לקרות ג
ולא וד בלבד אלא כל שאמרו חכמ'
עד חצות מצותן עד שיעלה
עמוד השחר ד הקטר
חלבים ואברים ואכילת פסחים
מצותן עד שיעלה עמוד השחר ה
כל הנאכלים ליום אחד
מצותן עד שיעלה עמוד השחר
ו אם כן למה אמרו חכמ' עד
חצות אלא להרחיק את האדם
מן העבירה ו מאמתי קורין
את שמע בשחרים משיכיר בין
תכלת ללבן ר' אלע' או' בין תכלת
לכרתי עד הנץ החמה ר' יהושע

אור' עד שלש שעות שכן דרך בני
מלכין לעמוד בשלש שעות הקורא
מכן ואילך לא הפסיד כאדם שהוא
קורא בתורה ה בית שמיי או'
בערב יטו ויקרו ובבקר יעמידו ועמ' וש'
בשכבך ובקומך בית הלל או' כל אדם
קורין כדרכן שנ' ובלכתך בדרך אם
כן למה נאמר בשכבך ובקומך אלא
בשעה שדרך שבני אדם שוכבים
ובשעה שדרך שבני אדם עומדין
ו אמר ר' טרפון אני הייתי בא בדרך
והטיתי לקרות כדברי בית שמיי וה'
וסכנתי בעצמי מפני הלסטיס אמרו
לו כדיי היית לחוב בעצמך שעברת
על דברי בית הלל ז בשחר
מברך שתים ואחת לאחריה
בערב מברך שתים לפניה ושתים לאחריה
אחת ארוכה ואחת קצרה מקום שאמרו
להאריך אינו רשיי לקצר לקצר לך אינו
רשיי להאריך לחתום אינו רשיי לחתום
שלא לחתום לחתום אינו רשיי לחתום
ח מזכירין יציאת מצרים
בלילות אמר ר' אלעזר בן עזריה הרי אני

3

50

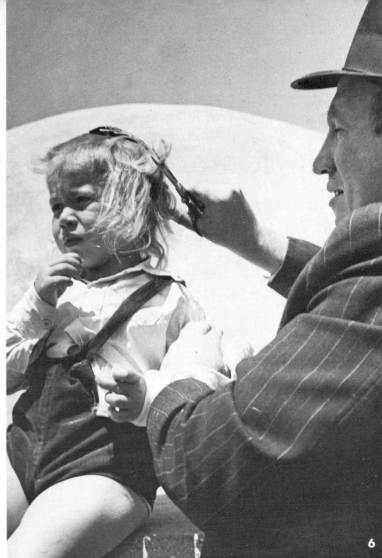

5

6

7

Motif: Sanhedrin in session; engraving, 1700–1704.
1. Restored necropolis at Bet She'arim, mishnaic-talmudic period, second–fourth centuries C.E.
2. Rabban Gamaliel, mishnaic sage, teaching; miniature in Italian *Haggadah*, c. 1300.
3. Mishnah text; the Kaufmann manuscript, 12th–14th centuries.
4. Joḥanan ben Zakkai leaves destroyed Jerusalem for Jabneh; Elkan, Knesset *menorah*.
5. Carvings of ritual objects in Bet She'arim catacomb.
6. Traditional haircutting on Lag ba-Omer at Meron, burial-place of Rabbi Simeon bar Yoḥai, scholar of the mishnaic period.
7. Tomb of his contemporary, Rabbi Meir, at Tiberias.

G E O N I M

Jews in
England

500   600   622   700 711   800   900   1000   1066

Muhammad's flight
to Medina

Arab conquest
of Spain

V I K I N G S

CHARLEMAGNE

Babylonia: The Two Yeshivot
The Talmud and the Geonim

Throughout the six centuries during which the Second Temple had stood in Jerusalem, a significant number of Jews had chosen to remain in the Babylonian exile. Indeed, a large area of Mesopotamia was almost exclusively populated by this community which became increasingly prosperous and enjoyed freedom of worship and autonomy. Babylonian Jewry was governed almost exclusively by the exilarch (Resh Galuta) who claimed descent from David. The community had maintained close and cordial relations with its co-religionists in Judah, it contributed to the upkeep of the Temple and, after its destruction, supported Bar Kokhba's revolt. It also sent many of its scholars to study in the Palestinian academies. At the same time, however, it developed independent institutions of law and learning. With the decline of the Palestinian schools, scholars streamed from Palestine to Mesopotamia.

One of the most brilliant of these was Abba Arikha (better known as Rav). In 219 C.E. he established an academy at Sura, while his colleague, Samuel, later founded a similar and rival institution at Nehardea. The latter, after its destruction by Palmarean forces in 261, was replaced by the school in Pumbedita. These academies ultimately became the religious authority for for the entire Jewish world of their time. Within their walls, Judah ha-Nasi's Mishnah was expanded and elucidated to include every imaginable circumstance. During their discussions, the students also touched on a fascinating variety of extraneous material. Thus the record of their debate (which was finally edited in the fifth century and is known as the Babylonian Talmud) contains far more than legal precepts. It constitutes a mirror of a complete civilization; it includes legends, stories and anecdotes, moral and ethical teachings, and investigations of natural and scientific matters. Together with the slightly earlier but less bulky Jerusalem Talmud produced in Judah, it thus provides an exemplar for a specific mode of learning and of living. The Talmud became canonized in Jewish esteem alongside the Bible and the Mishnah—theoretically in a descending scale of sanctity. In practice, interpretation of the Talmud and the talmudic mode of decision eventually dominated Jewish scholarship.

The heads of the two academies of Sura and Pumbedita came to enjoy a position almost equal to that of the exilarch. Known as the *Geonim*, they gave their name to the whole period. Even during the succeeding centuries of wider Jewish dispersion, these sages remained the ultimate authority on matters connected with Jewish law and religion. Their formulations of the liturgy, no less than their elucidations of the Talmud, became accepted throughout the Jewish world. By means of both written responsa and direct oral instruction, they exercised moral and social control over widespread Jewish communities. Sometimes a struggle over judicial, and even civil, prerogatives developed between individual *Geonim* and exilarchs. But far greater was the schism which took place in the ninth and tenth centuries between the *Geonim*, also known as the Rabbanites, and the Karaites. The latter sect, led by one Anan ben David, rebelled against the geonic attempt to establish the Talmud as the Book of Life for the Jewish people. Instead they insisted on a literal interpretation of the Scriptures and a primitive conception of Jewish ideals and duties. But, although they were much influenced by contemporary Islamic thought, they also represented an echo of sectarian tendencies of the Second Temple period. Their views were not overcome until Saadiah, the greatest of the *Geonim*, challenged the Karaites on their own ground. For the first time in Jewish history, this scholar embarked on a systematic attempt to place tradition on a rational, rather than a purely arbitrary basis.

But Saadiah's new scholarship was not to be continued by Mesopotamian Jewry. In the tenth and 11th centuries that community began to decline, primarily as a result of adverse political conditions. Jews continued to live in the area until modern times, when most immigrated to Israel. But their scholastic tradition had long since passed elsewhere.

2

3

4

Motif: Title page of tractate of Babylonian Talmud; Amsterdam, 1764.

1. Mosaic in the synagogue of Severus at Hammath near Tiberias, third-fourth centuries C.E.; relic of post-destruction Jewish life, talmudic period. The colorful illustrations, which are of a high artistic standard and in an excellent state of preservation, include (above) an Ark of the Law flanked by two seven-branched *menorot* and other ceremonial objects such as *lulavim*, *shofarot*, and incense shovels, and (below) the signs of the zodiac with their Hebrew names. The figure with the halo is a representation of Helios, the Greek sun god.

2-3-4. "If I Forget Thee, O Jerusalem!"

2. Temple's *menorah* remembered in third-century marble relief from Priene in Asia Minor.

3. Solomon's Temple represented by the exiles; one of the dozens of brightly colored murals found in the third-century synagogue at Dura-Europos, near the Euphrates.

4. Yearning for Zion; *Haggadah* illustration created by Saul Raskin to accompany Psalm 126: "When the Lord brought back those that returned to Zion, we were like unto them that dream . . . . They that sow in tears shall reap in joy."

5-6-7-8. Study of Babylonian Talmud in Yeshivot.

5. Lomza yeshivah in prewar Poland.

6. Eẓ Ḥayyim yeshivah; Jerusalem, 1949.

7. Porat Yosef, Sephardi yeshivah; Jerusalem, 1951.

8. Lubavitch ḥasidic yeshivah; Melbourne, Australia, 1973.

							Jews expelled from France		Jewish badge in Italy					Jews expelled from England	
1000					1100			1182		1200	1215				1290	1300

Magna Carta

C R U S A D E S

Marco Polo's travels

12
In Arabian Lands
A Protected People

Jewish communities existed in Arabia long before the advent of Islam. Some legends date the arrival of the first Jews to that area as early as the time of Moses; others tell of the arrival of 80,000 priests during the first Exile. These had ignored Ezra's call to return to Judaism. Instead, they had combined into powerful local tribes, which on occasion ruled subject peoples and won numerous converts. One sixth-century king of Yemen, Yusuf Dhu Nuwas, was himself converted. The extent of the continued Jewish influence in the area is demonstrated by the amount of Jewish history and legend in the Koran.

When Muhammad launched his new religion, he expected the Jews to accept it. His disappointment at their refusal ultimately caused him to change his initial policy of toleration towards them. Instead, the Jewish tribes of Arabia were assaulted; most were either expelled or forced to embrace Islam, all the male members of one tribe being put to death. Others, as in the Yemen, were permitted the privilege of remaining under Muslim rule on condition that they paid a heavy tribute and suffered numerous social indignities and economic restrictions. Their dress, occupations, and mode of transport were all governed by strict laws. As often happens, such necessities became virtues. The Yemenite Jews for example became specialist workers in silver and gold (occupations forbidden to Muslims). They also remained ethnically apart and preserved their distinctive customs. Thus their unique pronunciation of Hebrew and their ritual practices have probably remained unchanged for over 2,000 years.

This pattern of Muslim-Jewish relationship was followed in the other oriental communities which swiftly fell before the warriors of the new faith. The ancient Jewish community in Egypt, in particular, began to flourish again under Arab rule.

By 712 the crescent of Islam ruled from the borders of India to the slopes of the Pyrennees and thus united under its sway more than 90 percent of the existing Jewish population. This had farreaching consequences for the economic and social structure of the Jews. The Muslim respect for trade and denigration of agriculture continued to draw the Jews away from the villages and into urban occupations. Thus, wherever a new city arose or an old one developed, Jews formed large and enterprising merchant and craftsman communities, as in Basra and Baghdad in Iraq; Cairo-Fostat and Alexandria in Egypt; and Kairouan and Fez in the Magreb. Thus the foundation was laid for the variegated structure of Jewish economy and society in the Muslim city, a feature which existed almost until the total liquidation of Jewish communities in the Orient after the creation of the State of Israel.

Each of these communities was governed by the *dhimma* doctrine governing the rights of "the people of protection"—Jews and Christians. As set out in the so-called Covenant of Omar (formally ascribed to the year 637) they were subject to various restrictions and could be punished severely if found reviling the Prophet. But they were at least accorded the right to exist and to practice their religion. Many shades of faith other than Islam existed in the lands ruled by the Muslims. This fact saved the Jews there from the predicament of becoming the main, frequently even the sole, representatives of non-conformity—as they were in Christendom. The tone of toleration which consequently developed in Islamic lands was long after to remain a vital factor in Jewish history.

In Erez Israel, in particular, it provided a much-needed respite. There, ever since Christianity had become the official religion of the Roman Empire in 321, the small Jewish community had suffered a series of persecutions, expulsions and forced conversions. One Arab ruler, Omar II (717-720) also imposed severe restrictions on the Jews. But it was the period of Arab rule in general (634-1099) which saw such Jewish communities as Ramle and Tiberias grow and prosper. Little wonder therefore that during the Crusades (1099-1291) the Jews cooperated with the Muslims in their battles against the Christian invaders.

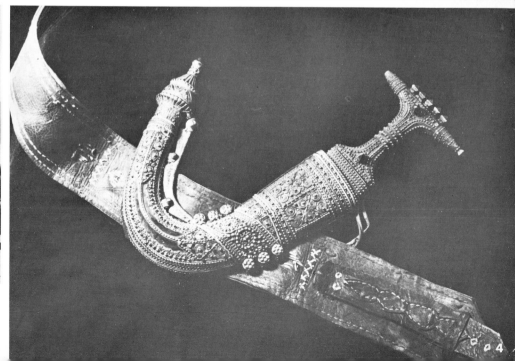

Motif: Abraham in Nimrod's fiery furnace; an aggadic theme represented in a Turkish Islamic work which was published c. 1583.

1. Yemenite Jews en route to Israel in the massive airlift known as Operation Magic Carpet, 1949, which transplanted virtually the whole of Yemen's Jewish population of 45,000.

2. Yemenite wedding, 1969, with bridal couple in traditional dress. The syncopated rhythm for the folk dancing is deftly tapped out on a kerosene tin.

3. Jewish inhabitants of the mellah of Agoin, in the Atlas Mountains of North Africa.

4. Filigree dagger worked by a Yemenite silversmith. The influx of Yemenite craftsmen to Israel stimulated the development of decorative metal-work.

5. Sir Moses Montefiore intercedes with the Sultan (on horseback) for Morocco's persecuted Jewry in the palace courtyard, 1863.

6. Sabbath afternoon scene in a Moroccan Jewish quarter, 19th century; from a painting attributed to Lecomte-Dunouy.

7. Interior of the Ben Ezra synagogue in Cairo, built c. 12th century, and showing strong Moorish influence.

	Armleder massacres	Black Death massacres			Censorship of Talmud			Expulsion from Spain

1300   1337   1348   1400   1415   1431   1492   1500

Joan of Arc

HUNDRED YEARS' WAR

Columbus discovers America

FERDINAND and ISABELLA

The Golden Age
Spain and its Influence

The Jews reaped the greatest benefits from Muslim rule in Spain. Under the Visigoths, the ancient Spanish Jewish community had suffered the full rigors of zealous Christian persecution. But after the Arab conquest of 711, Jews were allowed to enter every walk of life. Such communities as Cordova and Toledo became renowned for their commercial success, while individual Jews also specialized in such free professions as medicine, philosophy and astronomy. Those who proved particularly gifted even attained political eminence becoming, like Ḥisdai ibn Shaprut (10th century), the caliph's adviser. The 11th century witnessed the rise of many similar personalities. Some of these statesmen were also talented Jewish scholars. Thus, Samuel ha-Nagid was both a commander of Muslim armies, vizier of a Muslim king, and a great Hebrew poet, eminent talmudist and philosopher as well. These men supported whole galaxies of poets and scholars.

Thus the importance of Muslim Spain in Jewish history is not restricted to the political sphere; this was also a golden age of Jewish literature and thought. Medieval Spanish Jews were thoroughly conversant with the contemporary renaissance in Arabic thought and learning. Under its inspiration they produced some of the greatest Hebrew poetry, grammatical studies and hymnologies of all time. Moreover, the junction of the rediscovered Greek philosophers with Jewish tradition also produced the intellectual phenomenon of the 12th century, in the person of Moses ben Maimon. Writing mainly in Cairo, he produced a methodic and logical presentation of the mass of talmudic teaching (the *Mishneh Torah*). In his major philosophical work, *The Guide for the Perplexed* (written in Arabic) he also presented a completely rational philosophy of Judaism. Although his writings initially aroused vehement criticism they ultimately became pillars of Jewish thought.

During the early Christian reconquest (11th century) Spanish Jewry continued to enjoy toleration and renown. In the reign of Alfonso VI, Christian Castile even provided a refuge for Andalusian Jews seeking refuge from Almohadan fanaticism. There too, Jewish diplomats, financiers and physicians abounded. But the Church became increasingly intolerant of the existence of Jews in a Christian state. Moreover, with the slow but sure advance of the Cross against the Crescent, it became less important for Christian rulers to conciliate their Jewish minorities. Ultimately, the restrictions of the 12th century were succeeded by the persecutions of 1391. Under these circumstances complete Jewish communities accepted baptism, and individual Jews thereby ensured their continued predominance in Spanish life. In isolated instances, these "New Christians" became sincere adherents of their new faith. But in most cases they secretly continued to practice their ancient religion. They are known in history as Marranos, and due to their influence vestiges of Jewish observance can still be seen in many Spanish gentile families today. Not even baptism, however, could save Spanish Jewry. During the 15th century the Inquisition displayed its full range of brutality. In 1492 all Jews had either to convert to Christianity or to leave the newly united Spanish kingdom. Thereafter, no synagogue was opened with official recognition until 1967.

The refugees fled to Ereẓ Israel, North Africa, Italy, Holland and Turkey. There, despite continued restrictions and sporadic persecutions, they continued the political and scholastic tradition of their fathers. They produced viziers in Ottoman Turkey and international financiers in North Africa. It was one of the children taken to Ereẓ Israel from Spain, Joseph Caro (1488-1575) who was also responsible for the *Shulḥan Arukh*— the massive compilation of religious practice and jurisprudence which has remained the standard Jewish legal authority. As a group, the exiles also fostered the liturgy, practices, and even the Judeo-Spanish language (Ladino) of their homeland. The Sephardi tradition (a derivation of the Hebrew name for Spain) thus remained a numerically powerful and culturally vital force in Jewish life. It continues to be so today.

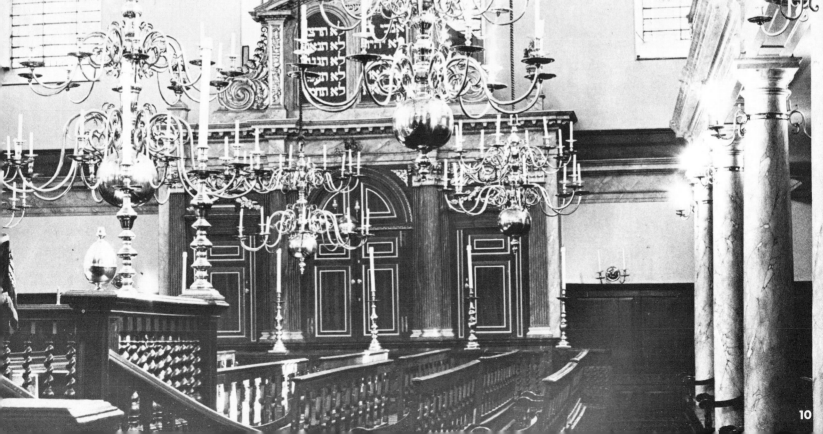

11

12

13

Motif: Moorish Ḥanukkah lamp; Spain, 15th century.

1. Procession of the Inquisition of Goa; 18th-century engraving.

2. The *Sanbenito*, dress of the "unrepentant" victims of the Spanish Inquisition, with demons and flames depicted on the tunic and miter.

3. Alfonso de Espina, harbinger of the Spanish Inquisition, followed by Jews who are shown blindfolded because "they do not see the truth." Spanish woodcut, c. 1474.

4. Statue of Solomon ibn Gabirol by U.S. sculptor Reed Armstrong, erected in Malaga, Spain.

5. Interior of the 14th-century Rambam (Maimonides) synagogue in Cordova.

6. The tomb of Maimonides in Tiberias.

7. Detail of the synagogue of Samuel ha-Levi Abulafia (later the El Transito Church) at Toledo, built c. 1357, showing alabaster grille on window and carved stucco decoration.

8. The Toledo synagogue founded in 1203; from 1411 the church of Santa Maria la Blanca.

9. The Portuguese Sephardi synagogue at Amsterdam, still standing; oil painting by Emmanuel de Witte, 1617–92.

10. The Bevis Marks Sephardi synagogue, London, founded 1701.

11. Title page of Maimonides' *Moreh Nevukhim*, Warsaw, 1872. The portraits represent the author (left), and Don Isaac Abrabanel, whose commentary appears in this edition.

12. Traditional portrait of Maimonides from Ugolinus' *Thesaurus Antiquitatum Sacrarum*, Venice, 1744.

13. Title page of Caro's *Shulḥan Arukh*, Mantua, 1722. The cartouches are imaginary portraits of the author and five of his classic commentators.

The Creation as depicted in the *Sarajevo Haggadah*, Spain, c. 1400. The top right panel shows the earth unformed and void. The next six panels show the six days of Creation: the division of light and darkness (first day); the division of the waters (second day); the creation of vegetation (third day); the creation of the sun and the moon (fourth day); the creation of living creatures (fifth day); and the creation of man (sixth day). The last panel, the Sabbath, is illustrated by a man resting. Throughout, the power of God is represented by rays of light.

The page below, from a Passover *Haggadah* written and illuminated in Altona-Hamburg in 1740 by Joseph bar David Leipnick of Moravia, ostensibly illustrates the labors of the Israelites in ancient Egypt. In fact, it shows contemporary Jews at work in a German town.

The forty years' wandering of the Israelites in the wilderness is commemorated by the festival of Sukkot. The "four species" used in the festive ritual—the citron, palm, myrtle and willow—are shown in the hands of an East European ḥasidic boy in "The Descendant of the High Priest" by Isidor Kaufmann, c. 1903.

Jebel Mūsā, one of the sites traditionally identified with Mt. Sinai, is named after an Arab Christian monk who lived there in the fourth century.

King David is shown playing the harp in an illuminated panel from the *Rothschild Miscellany*, Ferrara, c. 1470.

The Old City of Jerusalem as it is today, in an aerial view, looking south. The ancient City of David was situated on the hillside beyond the Temple Mount (where the gold-capped Dome of the Rock now stands), extending down toward the Valley of Siloam (upper left). At upper right may be seen Mt. Zion, which is thought by some to be the burial-place of King David. The Rockefeller Museum (in the foreground) houses many of the artifacts found by archaeologists.

The Prophet Ezekiel's vision of the valley of dry bones (Ezek. 37) is depicted in one of the murals in the third-century synagogue at Dura-Europos on the Euphrates. The painting, in the form of a continuous narrative, shows the hand of God setting Ezekiel down in the valley.

The lower illustration is a page from an anonymous travelogue known as the *Casale Pilgrim*, from Casale Monferrato, Italy, and dated 1758. The sketches seen here are stylized representations of the tombs of certain named Galilean scholars of the mishnaic period—the first and second centuries.

Tel Aviv's *Adloyada* carnival is one of the many events of the Purim festival which commemorates the miraculous redemption of the Jews of Persia in the First Temple period.

The scouts in the photograph below are about to kindle the Ḥanukkah torch at Modi'in, the home of the Hasmonean family which raised a successful revolt against the Seleucid invaders of Ereẓ Israel in the second century B.C.E. The torch is relayed by runners from the site of the Maccabean tombs to Jerusalem.

Among the relics of the Crusader occupation of Ereẓ Israel are the ruins of the fortress of Montfort in the Keziv Gorge in Upper Galilee. ►

The original 11th-century synagogue at Worms was destroyed by the Nazis in 1938 and reconstructed in 1961. Connected to it is the Rashi Chapel.

At Meron, in the Galilee, Ḥasidim dance around a bonfire on Lag ba-Omer, a minor festival linked with the name of the talmudic sage, Rabbi Simeon bar Yoḥai.

This "Description of the Land of Promise" by Tilemann Stella shows the Middle East from Egypt to Syria. The copper engraving was published by Abraham Ortelius in Antwerp in 1579.

"Ghetto Politicians" in an East European *shtetl* are shown in Lazar Krestin's painting, dated 1904.

The carved wooden doors shown above were salvaged from an 18th-century Polish synagogue and are preserved in the Sir Isaac and Lady Wolfson Museum in Jerusalem. The creatures illustrate the Hebrew inscription, which is an excerpt from a mishnaic dictum (Avot 5:23): "Be strong as a leopard, swift as an eagle, fleet as a deer, and brave as a lion, to do the will of thy Father in heaven."

The Joḥanan ben Zakkai Synagogue in the Jewish Quarter of the Old City of Jerusalem is named for the talmudic sage who, according to tradition, prayed on that spot during the Roman siege of the city. The masonry of the reconstructed building incorporates carved stones from the original 400-year-old edifice that was razed to the ground during the Jordanian occupation of the Old City. The mural above the ark, depicting the "heavenly Jerusalem," incorporates biblical quotations, including the oath of the Psalmist: "If I forget thee, O Jerusalem, let my right hand forget her cunning."

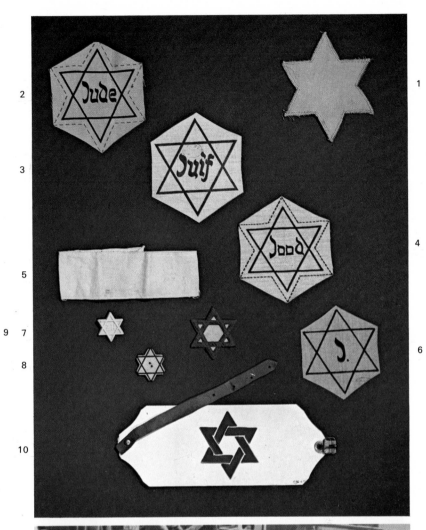

Discriminatory badges which European Jews were compelled to wear during the Nazi Occupation: 1. Bulgaria, Poland (part), Lithuania, Hungary, Greece (part); 2. Germany, Alsace, Bohemia-Moravia; 3. France; 4. Holland; 5. Greece, Serbia, Belgrade, Sofia; 6. Belgium; 7. Slovakia; 8. Bulgaria; 9. Slovakia; 10. Poland (part), East and Upper Silesia.

The postwar ingathering of the exiles included hundreds of thousands of Jews from Oriental countries, such as these Moroccan immigrants, awaiting their disembarkation at Haifa Port, 1961.

Israel's schoolchildren plant trees annually on Tu bi-Shevat, the traditional New Year of Trees. The above group is helping reclaim Arad, a biblical site in the northern Negev which is being turned into a thriving industrial town.

Soviet immigrants arriving at Lod Airport in 1972 get their first glimpse of the Promised Land.

Garlanded toddlers at Jerusalem's Independence Park celebrate Shavuot, the thanksgiving Festival of First Fruits, with baskets of newly-picked fruit and vegetables.

Torah Scrolls are carried in procession up the hills of Jerusalem to the Western Wall on Simḥat Torah, the Festival of the Rejoicing of the Law. The canopy, or *ḥuppah*, is the same as that used for the wedding ceremony, since the Torah is the marriage contract that binds God and the People of the Book.

Tanks pass the 16th-century walls of the Old City during Israel's 25th anniversary parade.

This *menorah*, symbol of the State of Israel, was executed by the Anglo-Jewish sculptor Benno Elkan, and presented by the British parliament to its Israel counterpart, the Knesset, in whose forecourt it stands. Each panel represents a significant episode in Jewish history.

Jewish Dress in the Lands of the Diaspora.

The leftmost ensemble is the North African *Kswat el Kabira* or "Grand Costume" given to a Jewish bride by her father for festive wear. Tracing its origin to the dress worn in Spain at the time of the Expulsion, it consists of five traditional parts: *jeltita*—a velvet fold-around skirt with bands of gold embroidery; *gonbaīz*—an open corselet with short sleeves; *punta* or *ktef*—a front worn inside the corselet; *kmam*—wide muslin sleeves fitting over the shoulders like a shawl; *hezam*—a girdle of gold lamé wound twice around the waist.

The vignettes, unless otherwise stated, date from the middle of the 19th century. Starting from the top left engraving on the opposite page, they represent respectively: a merchant and a member of the lower classes, both from Algeria; a burgher from The Hague; an 18th-century Polish Jew, wearing a black *kapote* with a sash under his cloak and a fur hat; a Dutch housewife; and a married woman from Algeria.

The two figures above represent (left) a Jewess from Constantinople, wearing a sleeveless Turkish *hyrka* over her dress and a large *fotoz* over her head; and (above right) a young Jewess from Algeria.

At right is seen a Bukharan bridal gown of cotton tulle, with characteristically Jewish spangled embroidery.

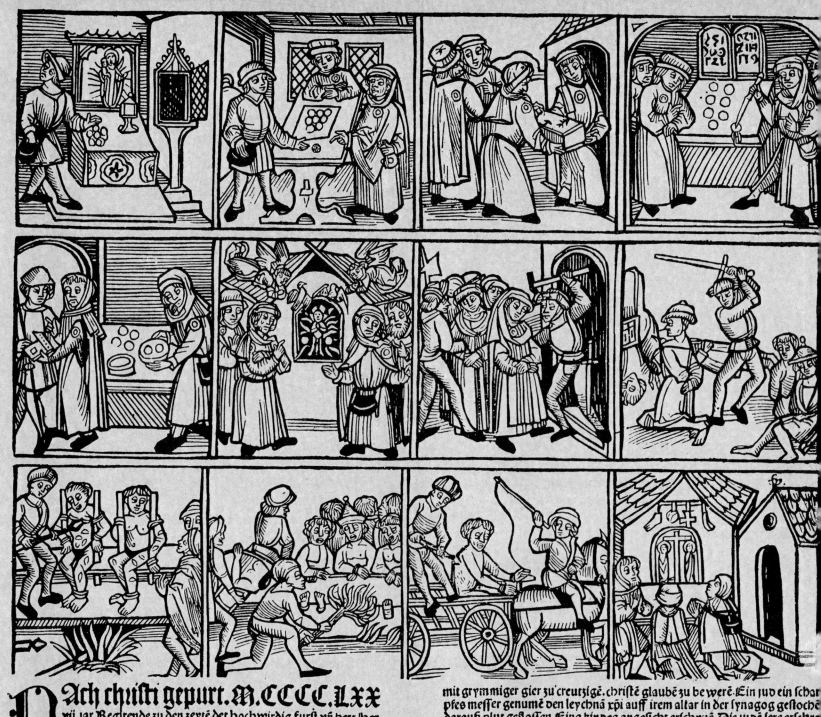

Ach christi gepurt. M.CCCC.LXX vij.iar Regirende zu den zeytē, der hochwirdig furst vō herr ser Vlrich zu passaw geborn vonn Nußdoiff. Es sat sych begeben das ein leychsertiger vū verzagter mensch weyland genant Cristoff eysengreißsamer / vergessende seiner sel selygkayt / nach Judas syten auß begyer

mit grymmiger gier zu creutzigē. christē glaubē zu be werē. Ein jud ein scharpfes messer genumē den leychnā xpi auff irem altar in der synagog gestochē darauß plut geslossen. Eins kindes angesicht erschynē. Die judē sere erschracken. wurdē zu radt. vū schicktē.ij. partickel gen Prag.ij. in die Newstat.ij. gen Saltzpurg.ij. partickel worffen sy yn einē glüendē packoffen. haben sy gesehen.ij.engel.ij.tauben auß dem ofen flygē. nachmals ist der vbelteiser

14

The Northern Centers
France and Germany

Jewish merchants first settled along the trade arteries of western Europe in Roman times. By the sixth century definable communities existed in Paris, Marseilles and Lyons. They subsequently pushed northeastwards into western Germany. There they were joined by such Italian families as the Kalonymids who had followed the routes of the Danube and the Elbe. Before long the Rhineland was thronged with thriving communities of international traders and local merchants. The authorities appreciated their talent and occasionally even invited Jews to settle in emerging urban areas. But, unlike the Spanish rulers, they did not admit them to society or government; instead the Rhineland Jews were classified as their rulers' private property and were barred from landowning and the professions. Thus, they were eventually forced into moneylending. Because the Church considered this to be an immoral occupation, the Jews were later persecuted for engaging in an activity originally imposed on them. Thus the figure of the Jewish extortionist became a widespread and longstanding obsession.

During the tenth and 11th centuries the Rhineland communities greatly enriched Jewish culture. Under their influence the Jewish religion now obtained a distinctly occidental branch. Here, the Talmud was studied with intensity and exactitude in numerous academies. Thus, Mainz produced Gershom ben Judah, known for his scholarship as "the Light of the Exile," and it was at Worms that the great Rashi (1040–1105) first studied the Bible and Talmud. His monumental commentary has ever since remained vital for the study of these works. With their sharp-witted students they set a standard of scholarship which their successors were proud to follow.

They were not allowed to do so in peace. The Rhineland communities stood athwart the path which the Crusaders took on their expeditions to liberate the Holy Land from the infidel. They were therefore the first to feel the full force of militant Christian zeal. Within a year of the proclamation of the First Crusade in 1095, whole communities had been either plundered, murdered, forcibly converted or expelled. Equally horrendous scenes were repeated during the second and third Crusades of the 12th century. This bloodthirsty religious mania proved infectious, especially during times of social or economic unrest. A tragic tradition of popular attacks on the Jews had been spawned. In the 13th century they were falsely, but consistently, accused of killing Christian children and using their blood for ritual purposes (the Blood Libel). In the 14th century they were automatically assumed to enter the churches in order to desecrate the Host. During the Black Death of 1348, in which a third of the European population died, they were also accused of poisoning the wells. Some of the greatest expressions of Christian religious art further nurtured this image of the Jew as a horrifying fiend, and this instigated succeeding generations.

Faced with such trials, the Jews found comfort and strength within their own beliefs and traditions. At one level they even welcomed the martyrdom forced on them, proclaiming *Kiddush Ha-Shem* to be the greatest virtue. In particular one group, known as Ḥasidei Ashkenaz, developed a distinctive type of pietism. Their teachings, which laid considerable stress on ethics and asceticism, also contained a great deal of demonology and other folk beliefs—no doubt due to the influence of the surrounding culture. At another level Jewish life became intensely inward-looking. Leadership of the communities increasingly devolved on the rabbi, and such charismatic figures as Meir ben Baruch of Rothenburg provided much-needed reassurance and guidance. At the same time the communities framed their own laws, which were occasionally coordinated with larger synods of inter-communal representatives. Together, these trends produced a cultural pattern considerably different from that of the Sephardim. Although glorying in the same beliefs, the Jews of Northern France and Germany (*Ashkenaz* in Hebrew) developed institutions, rituals and even a language (Yiddish) peculiar to themselves. Even today, Western Jews are known as Ashkenazim, being still under the influence of this age.

6   7   8

14

15

Motif: Detail from German broadsheet, c. 1480, recounting alleged desecration of the Host in Passau, Bavaria, in 1478.

1. The narrative proceeds from the sale of the stolen Eucharist wafers to the arrest and torture of the Jewish victims of the libel.

2. The synagogue at Worms, Germany, begun in 1034 and rebuilt in 1175; photographed before its destruction by the Nazis on *Kristallnacht*, 1938.

3. The *mikveh* (ritual bath) uncovered at Cologne, Germany, built in 1170.

4. The Gothic-style synagogue in Bamberg, Germany, built in the 13th century.

5. Jewish cemetery in Worms, established in 1076–77.

6. Jews in their distinctive hats receive charter of privileges from Emperor Henry VII in 1312; from *Codex Baldvini*, Koblenz.

7. Pillar from Kalonymus family residence, tenth century, Mainz, Germany. The eagle, insignia of the current ruler, was a mark of privilege.

8. Charter of privileges granted by Charles V to the Jews of Worms, 1551.

9. Crusader fortress at Caesarea, Erez Israel, built 1251.

10. Synagoga, the medieval Christian personification of Judaism, with fallen crown, broken staff, and eyes blindfolded by a serpent; Eglise St. Seurin in Bordeaux, 1264.

11. Crowned stone figure of Ecclesia, representing Christianity, with banner aloft.

12. Christian resorting to Jewish moneylender; woodcut, Strasbourg, 1541.

13. Jewish family burned at the stake; from "The Profanation of the Host," a series of panels painted by Paolo Uccello c. 1468 for a church in Urbino.

14. *Concerning the Jews and their Lies*, anti-Semitic pamphlet by Martin Luther, Wittenburg, 1543.

15. The blood libel revived; Julius Streicher's Nazi newspaper *Der Stürmer*, May 1934.

16. Soldiers break into home of Jew accused of desecration of Host; panel by Uccello.

16

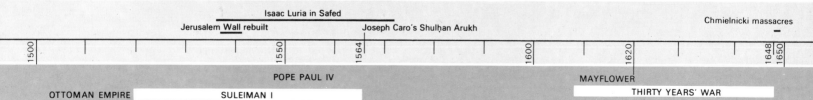

15

Eastern Europe
Persecution and Autonomy

Despite the persecutions and expulsions of the Middle Ages some Jews continued to live in northern Europe. Some towns, having hastily expelled their Jews for ostensibly religious motives, ultimately invited them back for plainly economic reasons. Moreover the political fragmentation of Germany precluded a general order of expulsion from that country, as had been issued in England in 1290 and in France in 1306. Nevertheless, the demographic axis of Ashkenazi Jewry moved eastwards into Poland-Lithuania.

That area already possessed a tradition of toleration. In 740 C.E. the king of the Khazars—a sovereign Turkic group—had adopted Judaism and his successors corresponded with the outside world of Rabbanite and Karaite Judaism. Until its destruction by the Slavs in the 10th century, a state controlled by a Jewish aristocracy had thus ruled the strategically important region between the Volga and the Caspian Sea. The later kings of Greater Poland were not motivated by theology. They welcomed the refugees from Germany not for their faith, but because they needed Jewish finance and commerce in order to develop the trade and industry of their newly settled lands. They therefore gave the Jews every encouragement to indulge their business acumen and allowed them unrestricted domicile throughout the realm. The migrants, in turn, entered most spheres of economic activity and became the dominant element of the "third estate." The richer among them were—progressively—moneylenders, merchants, manufacturers, tax farmers, and stewards and administrators of the great estates. The poorer became peddlers, craftsmen, innkeepers and farmers. Poland thus became the land of financial promise and numerical predominance for Ashkenazi Jewry.

It was also the land of model Jewish self-government. This period witnessed the emergence of the predominantly Jewish township and of a lifestyle which was later to reach its apogee in the *shtetl* (small town) of Czarist Russia. In western Europe the area of segregated Jewish settlement (the ghetto) had been imposed by the Christian authorities in order to close the Jews in. In eastern Europe it was a useful device which the Jews themselves fostered for keeping alien influences out. There, Yiddish remained the dominant language of speech and (increasingly) of literature, and there the nature of life became as essentially Jewish as the inhabitants themselves. The synagogue and the school were supreme, the sense of religious solidarity was all-pervading, and the governing body of the community omnipotent. This was especially true at a national level. In 1551 the Jews of Poland were permitted to elect their chief rabbi and judges, who were to exercise jurisdiction in all matters concerning Jewish law. During the same century, the separate communities of the four provinces of Poland-Lithuania also began to elect a unified governing body, known as the Council of the Lands. Consisting of delegates from all the important Jewish communities, it usually met twice a year during the major trade fairs and acted as both legislator and executive. The Council apportioned taxes, enforced royal edicts, imposed sanctions, and decided disputes between communities and between individuals. Under its aegis the Jews of Poland formed in all but name a state within a state.

Characteristically, scholastic achievements mirrored advances in other spheres. Indeed Polish Jewry placed a greater emphasis on mass education than anywhere else in the Jewish world; the sheer number of Polish yeshivah students, and their average quality, surpassed even the standard formerly attained in Germany. They produced many of the major works in rabbinic literature and developed new methods in the study of Talmud.

But Polish Jewry's hour of glory was brief. In 1648 the Ukrainian Cossacks under Bogdan Chmielnicki revolted against their Polish masters. They also released the floodgates of popular opposition to the position which the Jews had enjoyed under royal favor. The result was a wave of pogroms, unprecedented in their viciousness and butchery, which devastated whole communities. Thousands of Jews were tortured and murdered, or fled. Those who remained were plunged into despair.

Motif: The 17th-century wooden synagogue of Chodorow, Poland. Scores of similar synagogues were burnt down by the Nazis on *Kristallnacht*, the "night of broken glass," November 9–10, 1938.

1. "Marketplace in Town," an evocative oil painting by Joseph Budko, 1930.

2. "Old Jewish Peddler," by Geskel Salomon; oil painting, 19th century, personifying the pathos and world-weariness of the eternally Wandering Jew.

3. "Wedding in Shtetl," oil painting by Saul Raskin, 1956. At left may be seen members of the *klezmer*, the township's spirited amateur ensemble.

4. Goose market at Cracow, early 19th century.

5. Jewish merchants at Cracow market; etching by A. Hervieu, 19th century.

6. "The Water-Carrier at the Town Well," *shtetl* scene by Maurycy Minkowski, 1927.

7. "Examination," by Isidore Kaufmann (1854–1921). The East European tradition of learning is epitomized in the domestic ritual of testing the young yeshivah student's progress in his Torah studies every Sabbath afternoon.

8. Judicial autonomy in the Diaspora; a medieval *bet din* in session, from an illuminated manuscript of Jacob ben Asher's legal code *Arba'ah Turim*, Mantua, 1435.

9. Lithuanian folk art; carved wooden ark in a 16th-century synagogue in Utena.

10. "The Cossacks are Coming," eyewitness drawing by Abel Pann, 1926.

11. Statue in Kiev of Bogdan Chmielnicki, who is still a Ukrainian national hero.

Jews readmitted to England

Jews arrive in America   Spinoza excommunicated

SHABBETAI ZEVI

Jewish expulsion from Vienna

1650   1654   1656   1670   1700

OLIVER CROMWELL

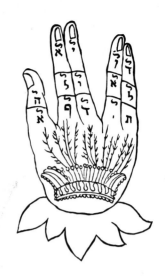

16
Spiritual Upheaval
Mysticism, Messianism and Ḥasidism

Ever since the second Exile, Jewish tradition has harbored two contrasting elements. The first, which was usually dominant, was the essentially practical sphere of talmudic study—instructing a man how to behave. The other was a mystical element (known as the Kabbalah) which attempted to fathom the manner in which God ruled. The latter, although more subdued, was never absent from Jewish tradition. Its influence is particularly marked in the apocalyptic books written prior to the destruction of the Second Temple, in the belief of many sectarian groups at that time, and in the Zohar, a mystical commentary on the Pentateuch which, although not discovered until the 13th century, was purportedly written over 1,000 years earlier. This mystical trend also fostered the belief in the coming of the Messiah and ultimate salvation. This tenet, despite the obscurity of its origin, has become basic to Judaism.

Not unexpectedly, concern with the Messiah—the date of his coming and the nature of his mission—was especially prevalent when the vicissitudes of ordinary existence deprived Jews of all other hope. Indeed every major wave of persecution aroused messianic expectation and messianic movements, which sometimes promised even reunifications with the descendants of the Ten Lost Tribes. Thus, early in the 16th century, the oppressed Jews of Asia Minor and Rome were stirred by the charismatic promises of David Reuveni and Solomon Molcho. During this period too, the study of the Zohar reached new heights, especially under the influence of Isaac Luria (1534–1572), the great mystic of Safed in Ereẓ Israel. All over the world students pored over his writings in the hope of forecasting the moment of messianic deliverance.

The Chmielnicki massacres of 1648-49 further stimulated this trend. Indeed, because these tribulations were of unprecedented ferocity, they gave rise to a messianic movement of unprecedented extent. In 1665-66 whole communities both in the orient and in Europe frenziedly sold their houses, possessions and businesses, and prepared to answer the call issued by one Shabbetai Ẓevi (1626-1676). Proclaiming himself the messiah who would return his people to the Holy Land, this Jew from Smyrna acted as though he were already their anointed king. He also set out to convince the sultan of Turkey of his fantastic claim. But there the dream collapsed. When the Ottoman authorities faced him with the alternative of apostasy or death, the "messiah" converted to Islam. Some of his followers continued to believe that this "descent" was an evanescent but necessary preliminary to a glorious rise. Shabbetai's cult, therefore, survived his death and even in the 18th century aroused vehement controversies in the rabbinical world. In eastern Europe it was encouraged by another self-proclaimed messiah, Jacob Frank (1726–1791). He emulated Shabbetai's example by converting to Christianity.

In the aftermath of this wave of hope and then despair Ḥasidism was born. Initially this revivalist movement attempted to infuse Jews with renewed faith in God's deliverance. It stressed the ability of every man, however ignorant and however poor, to communicate with his Maker. It thus constituted a revolt against the hegemony of scholarship. The masses flocked to hear the disciples of Israel Ba'al Shem (c. 1700-1760), the acknowledged founder of the movement, proclaim that God could best be served in joy and gladness. The fierce opposition which the movement aroused largely stemmed from a fear that the Shabbatean heresy was repeating itself. Particularly, Elijah the Gaon of Vilna (1720-1797), the greatest scholar of the age, encouraged an edict of excommunication against its adherents. For a time, eastern European Jewry was therefore divided between Ḥasidim and Mitnaggedim (opponents). Nevertheless, Ḥasidism did not develop into a sectarian movement. Its ideas have had an enduring effect on Judaism. Some hasidic *rebbes* were amongst the first religious leaders to proclaim the duty of settlement in the Holy Land. Others remained in eastern Europe, where they greatly stimulated Jewish life. Their traditions are today continued in Israel and the U.S.A.

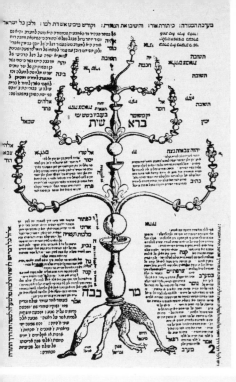

92

9

10

11

12

Motif: Hand depicted as a mystical symbol in a kabbalistic work published in Hanau in 1612.

1. Ḥasidim dance with mystical fervor on Lag ba-Omer at Meron in the Galilee. The toddlers on their fathers' shoulders are about to have their first haircut.

2. *Menorah* with kabbalistic allusions and quotations; from a Hebrew broadsheet by the French Christian kabbalist Guillaume Postel, Venice, c. 1548.

3. Elijah, harbinger of the Messiah, greeted during the Passover *Seder* service; from *Washington Haggadah*, Italy, 15th century.

4. Shabbetai Ẓevi (1626–1676), false messiah.

5. Jacob Frank (1729–1791), false messiah.

6. Imaginary depiction of miraculous messianic revelations surrounding Shabbetai Ẓevi; German engraving, 18th century.

7. Members of the Galilean moshav Kefar Ḥasidim, photographed in 1925. Its founders, Ḥasidim from Poland led by two rabbis, drained malarial swamps and established a farming settlement.

8. "Ḥasidim in a Bet Midrash," an oil painting by Isidor Kaufmann. The tablet to the left of the women's gallery gives the text of Psalm 24, which extols "him that hath clean hands and a pure heart."

9. Elijah, the Gaon of Vilna, chief opponent of Ḥasidism.

10. Lubavitcher Ḥasid from Russia.

11. Gur Ḥasidim in distinctive Sabbath garb stroll to Western Wall. The high fur hat is known as a *spodek*.

12. Young Ḥasidim dance with abandon at the Simḥat Bet ha-Sho'evah celebrations in Jerusalem during the festival of Sukkot.

GAON OF VILNA

BA'AL SHEM TOV

| 1700 | | | | | | 1750 | | | 1773 | | | | 1800 |

VOLTAIRE   SEVEN YEARS' WAR   Boston Tea Party   FRENCH REVOLUTION

PETER THE GREAT   AMERICAN WAR OF INDEPENDENCE

17

New Winds
The Enlightenment

While the Jews of Poland-Lithuania thus created a new stream within Judaism, those in western Europe forged a new type of Jew. Their efforts were made possible by changes within the political structure of medieval European society. By the late 17th century the loose-knit conglomerations dominated by conservative corporations were being replaced by the aggressive and mercantilist absolute states. The principal method by which the absolute monarchs planned to rule their lands was centralization; and they were therefore determined to curtail the autonomy of the Jews as a group. But their principal goal was power; and to attain this they were equally anxious to exploit the usefulness of the Jew as an individual. The Jew possessed the commercial tradition and international contacts necessary for the promotion of national trade and industry. He also owed loyalty to no rival group within the realm.

The result was a social transformation. By the end of the 17th century increasing numbers of German princes employed Jews as court financiers, purveyors and administrators, even encouraging select Jewish immigration to obtain these valuable assets. The majority of central European Jewry, of course, remained despised and downtrodden. But a select few became privileged and protected Court Jews. As such, they were permitted to dress, behave and live like normal members of society. Some Court Jews fell as suddenly and dramatically as they had risen, but others (on occasions) successfully interceded on behalf of their less-favored co-religionists. They thus exercised a dominant influence on Jewish life, especially in Germany. The Court Jew became the commanding communal figure, wielding an influence which superseded even that of the rabbi. He also created an example of apparently successful integration with secular society which other Jews craved to imitate. His sons aspired to a university education and his daughters to the patronage of artistic salons. They thus took the leap from social to cultural aspirations.

An intellectual phenomenon named Moses Mendelssohn

(1729-1786) instructed them how to do so. He was as conversant with German as with Jewish culture, and attempted to familiarize his people with the supposedly complementary beauties of both. He stressed the importance of secular education in Jewish schools, of "creative" crafts as Jewish occupations, and of Hebrew and German (rather than Yiddish) in Jewish learning. Significantly, his movement was known as the Haskalah (Enlightenment). In eastern Europe it was to pave the way for a remarkable revival of Hebrew letters.

In Germany itself, Mendelssohn's efforts produced various and varied reactions. At one extreme, his followers (and his children) carried his principles to their logical conclusion. Unlike Mendelssohn himself they were unable to withstand the social temptations and psychological pressures of the dominant culture, and many became apostates. They thus confirmed the worst fears of the traditional rabbis, most of whom had vehemently opposed Mendelssohn's theories. Another group of Mendelssohn's disciples took the more restricted path of a drive for change within Judaism itself. Originally, this began as a movement for superficial changes in synagogal worship. Ultimately it developed into a general revolt against all traditional forms. By the middle of the 19th century a complete philosophy of Reform Judaism evolved, repudiating much of the rabbinic structure and the talmudic Judaism on which it was based. This, in turn, had the effect of stimulating the traditionalist-minded to re-examine the intellectual basis of their own beliefs, and gave birth to the Conservative Judaism of Zacharias Frankel and the neo-orthodoxy of Samson Raphael Hirsch. Simultaneously, these groups evolved a new and vitally important Science of Judaism. Using the modern tools of criticism and the modern institution of the Theological Seminary, they conducted a rational investigation of Jewish history, law, literature and ritual. They thus opened avenues of academic, no less than theological, enquiry which are still being profitably pursued today in America and Israel.

Der Talmud
in seiner Nichtigkeit

dargestellt.

Von

A. Buchner,

Lehrer der hebräischen Sprache und der heiligen Schrift
an der Rabbinerschule zu Warschau.

עמי מאשריך מתעים: (ישעיהו ג' י"ב)

Mein Volk, die dich leiten, verführen dich. (Jef. 3, 12.)

Zweiter Theil.

———————

Warschau,
gedruckt in der Miffions-Druckerei, Eifengaffe Nr. 2449.
1848.

11

Motif: Rise and fall of an emancipated Jew; Joseph Suess Oppenheimer (1698/99–1738), financial adviser to the duke of Wuerttemberg, and the iron cage in which his body was exhibited after his execution.

1. Temple of the North Shore Reform congregation of Glencoe, Illinois, designed by Minura Yamasaki; a departure from conventional concepts of synagogue architecture.

2. Samuel Oppenheimer (1630–1703), Austrian Court Jew, whose contemporaries nicknamed him *Judenkaiser.*

3. Daniel Itzig (1723–1799), banker, entrepreneur and leader of Berlin Jewish community.

4. Abraham Geiger (1810–1874), early German Reform rabbi, philologist and historian.

5. Leopold Zunz (1794–1886), historian, a founder of the "Science of Judaism."

6. Samuel Holdheim (1806–1860), a pioneer of Reform Judaism, whose Berlin congregation held its weekly services on Sundays.

7. Heinrich Heine (1797–1856), German Jewish lyrical poet and essayist.

8. Dorothea von Schlegel (1763–1839), German authoress, apostate daughter of Moses Mendelssohn.

9. Adolf Jellinek (1820/21–1893), Vienna preacher and Haskalah scholar.

10. Etching of Moses Mendelssohn (left) with his friend Gotthold Lessing (standing) and Johann Lavater, the Lutheran theologian who challenged him to apostatize.

11. Title page of a radical Haskalah work, *Der Talmud in seiner Nichtigkeit* ("The Talmud in its Emptiness") by Abraham Buchner, Warsaw, 1848. In this copy, an outraged reader has amended the initial letter of the offending word from 'N' to 'W', so that instead of "Emptiness" the last word of the title is now "Importance."

Sanhedrin

HASKALAH

1800 1807 1847 1848 1869 1880

NAPOLEON I

California Gold Rush
Marx's Communist Manifesto

CRIMEAN WAR Suez Canal opened Telephone
invented

AMERICAN CIVIL WAR

RUSSIA NICHOLAS I ALEXANDER II

18

The Promise of Emancipation
Toleration or Equality

At the very moment that the Jews of western Europe embarked on such strenuous efforts to accommodate themselves to their gentile environment, their hosts were making equally novel attempts to accept the Jews as equals. Ever since the 16th century Reformation had destroyed the unity of Christendom, the Jews had ceased to be the only non-conformists in a culture of total agreement. The way was thus opened for the first hesitant steps towards toleration, which found particular expression in the re-admittance of the Jews to England in 1656 by Cromwell's Puritan regime. The later movement of European Enlightenment also stressed the proven merits of every individual, rather than the supposed inamicability of his race. Some of the enlightened despots, often the very rulers who employed Court Jews, occasionally implemented these ideas. Such efforts were further encouraged by the achievements of Moses Mendelssohn.

But while many gentiles thus defended the rights of individual Jews to toleration, very few supported their continued existence as a separate group. This dilemma re-appeared during the French Revolution when the rights of the "good" Sephardi Jews of the south of the country were more readily acknowledged than those of the "uncivilized" communities of Alsace-Lorraine. Admittedly Robespierre and his followers, after prolonged debate, did finally carry through full emancipation as a matter of revolutionary logic in 1791. But the same logic demanded that emancipation be granted only to Jews as individuals—in practice, only to Jews ready and willing to leave their own culture and assimilate with the French. Napoleon Bonaparte consummated this philosophy. In 1806 he convened an assembly of Jewish notables and, later, a Sanhedrin. He required that the assembled representatives of French, Italian and German Jewry define their claims to Napoleon's limited offer of civil equality. The only way in which they could do so was by asserting their undying patriotism to the fatherland and by relinquishing their aspirations to a separate national existence.

Ultimately, the French armies proved more beneficial to the Jews than did the French legislature. Napoleon's whirlwind conquests of central Europe were everywhere accompanied by the fall of the ghettos, whose denizens were suddenly dazzled by emancipation decrees. Holland in 1796, Venice in 1797, Rome in 1798 and Westphalia in 1807 all granted Jews full citizenship, as did Prussia (independently of direct French pressure) in 1812. This process continued, albeit with periodic interruptions after Napoleon's fall. In England, the struggle for emancipation culminated in 1858 when Lord Nathan Rothschild was finally allowed to take his seat in parliament as a professing Jew. In France, the last Jewish disabilities were abrogated through the influence of Adolphe Crémieux, a French Jewish statesman, in 1846. He also obtained the decree conferring equality on the Jews of Algeria in 1870. In the same year Jews were granted equal civil rights throughout the newly united countries of Italy and Germany.

The political emancipation enacted by the European legislators was meanwhile accompanied by the social emancipation resulting from economic changes on the continent. The Jews did not create the Industrial Revolution, but they certainly helped it to spread. The mere name of Rothschild sufficiently illustrates the part played by Jewish financiers, who were gradually joined by a galaxy of merchants, industrialists, inventors and entrepeneurs all over Europe. But no less significant is the fact that, with the increasing equality of opportunity, the field of Jewish enterprise was considerably widened. The Jews now became prominent in medicine, law, journalism, literature, art, science and even politics. In the process many forsook their faith—in numbers which sometimes reached the proportions of a mass movement. But others remained proud of their tradition. With Benjamin Disraeli loudly proclaiming his Jewish ancestry in the British parliament, with Adolphe Crémieux a member of the French cabinet, and with Ferdinand Lasalle the leader of the Social Democrat movement in Germany, it seemed that Jewish achievements could know no bounds.

2

DÉPÔT DES LOIS, À PARIS.

N° 576.   Bulletin des Lois, n° 198.

DÉCRET IMPÉRIAL

Concernant les Juifs qui n'ont pas de nom de famille et de prénoms fixes.

À Bayonne, le 20 juillet 1808.

NAPOLÉON, EMPEREUR DES FRANÇAIS, ROI D'ITALIE, et PROTECTEUR DE LA CONFÉDÉRATION DU RHIN;

Sur le rapport de notre ministre de l'intérieur,

Notre Conseil d'État entendu,

Nous AVONS DÉCRÉTÉ et DÉCRÉTONS ce qui suit:

ARTICLE PREMIER.

Ceux des sujets de notre Empire qui suivent le culte hébraïque, et qui, jusqu'à présent, n'ont pas eu de nom de famille et de prénoms fixes, seront tenus d'en adopter dans les trois mois de la publication de notre présent décret, et d'en faire la déclaration par-devant l'officier de l'état civil de la commune où ils sont domiciliés.

2. Les Juifs étrangers qui viendraient habiter dans l'Empire, et qui seraient dans

3

4

5   6

Is it not Written, Your Nation shall be a scab a scorn a spitting; & would You sit in the House of C——s?

Mine goot friend, it ish possiable to sit there, midout spoiling Your Propheshie.

JEWISH DISABILITYS

Motif: Medal struck by Abraham Abramson, 1808, in honor of the Napoleonic emancipation of the Jews of Westphalia.

1. Session of the Grand Sanhedrin convened in Paris by Napoleon in 1806 to ratify the ideological conditions of his proposed partial emancipation of the Jews.

2. *Naturalisationspatent*, the document conferring full citizenship on Daniel Itzig, the first Prussian Jew to be so honored; dated May 2, 1791.

3. Napoleonic decree requiring the Jews of France to adopt definitive family and first names; dated July 20, 1808.

4. Bronze medal commemorating Napoleon's Sanhedrin, dated May 30, 1806. The pose of the Jewish figure is significant.

5. Isaac Adolphe Crémieux, French statesman, and the first Jewish lawyer to successfully resist the requirement of taking the humiliating anti-Semitic oath *more judaico*, in 1817.

6. Helvetia, Switzerland personified, is petitioned for protection by her Jewish subjects; an engraving dating from 1765.

7. Baron Lionel de Rothschild takes his seat in the House of Commons (July 28, 1858), the first Jew to do so; from *The Illustrated London News*.

8. The Carlton Club toasts Benjamin Disraeli, Lord Beaconsfield; from *The Illustrated London News*, August 3, 1878.

9. Clergyman and portly Jew discuss the admission of Jews to the House of Commons during the 1830 debate on emancipation in England; lithograph from *The Looking Glass*, a satirical broadsheet.

RUSSIAN POGROMS

BILU

FIRST ALIYAH

1880

1882

1890

1900

BISMARCK IN GERMANY

RUSSIA

ALEXANDER III

NICHOLAS II

19
The New World
Freedom from Oppression

But the greatest land of Jewish promise in the 19th century was America. Ever since Christopher Columbus had—with considerable Marrano help—discovered the vast continent in 1492, Jews have been numbered amongst its settlers. The first immigrants were Sephardim; Spanish and Portuguese refugees in the West Indies, and Dutch merchants on the mainland. They were slowly followed by new arrivals from Germany and Poland. After the peace of Vienna (1815) the Ashkenazi trickle became a flood. By the mid-19th century the vast majority of American Jews spoke English with a German accent, when not speaking their native German. Following the trail of the Gold Rush of 1849 they spread throughout the country establishing rudimentary congregations in almost every incipient city and township from New York to San Francisco. In these, many followed the traditional paths of Orthodox Jewry. But others took the opportunity to give free reign to the new trends in Judaism which were gaining ground in western Europe. Vigorously led from Cincinnati by Isaac Meir Wise (1818–1900), an extreme type of Reform Judaism struck particularly deep roots. As a common meeting ground, the immigrants in 1843 established the "Independent Order of Benei Brith," which within a century became an organization of world-wide importance.

Such progress had taken place against a background of egalitarianism without parallel elsewhere in the world. The new land was uncontaminated by traditions of oppressive practices against the Jews and their emancipation had come as part of the independence and liberation of the American states. Thus 1776 was an important date in Jewish history too. In that year for the first time, the equality of peoples of all religions was accepted as a matter of principle and of fact. Even the earliest American Jews were thus encouraged to play a full part in American life. Some had fought for the colonists during the War of Independence and several thousand of their descendants battled on both sides during the Civil War.

In the 1880s, the coincidence of the labor famine in America and the outbreak of pogroms in eastern Europe brought a dramatically sudden increase of Jewish immigration to America in which over two and a half million East European Jews crossed the Atlantic ocean between 1881 and 1914. They settled principally in the eastern states—with New York especially becoming a major point of Jewish concentration. But enormous communities also sprang up in such other vast urban "melting pots" as Chicago, San Francisco and, across the Canadian border, in Toronto and Montreal. There, Yiddish became a common language of speech and print; there, numerous synagogues and educational institutions—of all sizes and every degree of orthodoxy—became common sights. Almost overnight, the axis of Jewish demography began to shift westwards. Despite the restricted U.S. immigration law of 1924 this trend was accentuated, in a particularly macabre way, by the Holocaust. In 1937 over 25% of world Jewry lived in the U.S.A.; in 1945 50% did so.

By then the community of newcomers had been succeeded by an enormously successful second generation. The majority of the latter were native-born, and in many cases their process of acculturalization had been accelerated by service in the U.S. army during both World Wars. The second generation entered almost every branch of industrial, professional and artistic enterprise. The American cinema, no less than its clothing industry, was indelibly stamped with their imprint.

Yet American Jewry was not so completely immersed in its own success that it could not spare more than a thought for less fortunate communities elsewhere. Even the earliest immigrants had scraped together a few cents to send back home, or had banded together in friendly societies to make their former townsmen welcome. Subsequently these activities became increasingly organized, increasingly varied and increasingly important. American Jewry became the principal patron of Jewish learning and the predominant provider of Jewish charity.

THE NEW COLOSSUS.

NOT LIKE THE BRAZEN GIANT OF GREEK FAME,
WITH CONQUERING LIMBS ASTRIDE FROM LAND TO LAND;
HERE AT OUR SEA-WASHED, SUNSET GATES SHALL STAND
A MIGHTY WOMAN WITH A TORCH, WHOSE FLAME
IS THE IMPRISONED LIGHTNING, AND HER NAME
MOTHER OF EXILES. FROM HER BEACON-HAND
GLOWS WORLD-WIDE WELCOME; HER MILD EYES COMMAND
THE AIR-BRIDGED HARBOR THAT TWIN CITIES FRAME,
"KEEP ANCIENT LANDS, YOUR STORIED POMP!"
        CRIES SHE
WITH SILENT LIPS. "GIVE ME YOUR TIRED, YOUR
        POOR,
YOUR HUDDLED MASSES YEARNING TO BREATHE FREE,
THE WRETCHED REFUSE OF YOUR TEEMING SHORE.
SEND THESE, THE HOMELESS, TEMPEST-TOST TO ME,
I LIFT MY LAMP BESIDE THE GOLDEN DOOR!"

⟵————————

THIS TABLET, WITH HER SONNET TO THE BARTHOLDI STATUE
OF LIBERTY ENGRAVED UPON IT, IS PLACED UPON THESE WALLS
IN LOVING MEMORY OF
EMMA LAZARUS
BORN IN NEW YORK CITY, JULY 22ᴰ 1849
DIED NOVEMBER 19ᵀᴴ, 1887.

8

THE MOST CROWDED SPOT IN AMERICA, NEW YORK'S GHETTO.

9

10

11

16

Motif: Replica of flag given to Abraham Lincoln in 1860 by an admirer, Abraham Kohn, with exhortation from Joshua 1:9—"Be strong and of good courage."

1. "Jewish Refugees from Russia passing the Statue of Liberty;" engraving by C. J. Staniland, 1892.

2. Orange vendor in New York, 1895.

3. Main Street in Salt Lake City, Utah, 1869; storefront at left bears name of Jewish merchant, N. S. Ransohoff.

4. Jackson, California, in the 1880s; contemporary painting by Ivy Mace Yarrington. One of the small buildings at left was the township's synagogue.

5. Sale of *mazzah* in New York shortly after the Civil War; engraving from *Frank Leslie's Popular Monthly.*

6. Jewish casualties in the Union forces at the Battle of Fredericksburg, December 13, 1862; part of list published in *The Jewish Record*, New York.

7. Immigrants passing through the Ellis Island depot at the turn of the century.

8. Sonnet by Emma Lazarus (1849–87) at the foot of the Statue of Liberty.

9. Cover of *Frank Leslie's Popular Weekly*, New York, April 23, 1903, showing the corner of Orchard and Ludlow streets on New York's Lower East Side, the main shopping area for Jews at the time.

10. "Going to the Synagogue," by Jacob Epstein, in *The Spirit of the Ghetto*, 1902.

11. Drawing by Jacob Epstein of a Lower East Side *ḥeder* for afternoon religious classes.

12. Sidewalk shop for religious requisites, Lower East Side; note small placard on top of showcase at right.

13. Advertisements from the Yiddish newspaper *Forward*, June 13, 1920. Many of them publicize relief activities organized by *landsmannschaften*, fraternities of townsfolk with a common place of origin.

14. Mayor Fiorello La Guardia (center) greets actor Solomon Mikhoels (left) and poet Itzik Feffer (right) during their visit to New York on behalf of the Soviet Anti-Fascist Committee, July 1943.

15. Voting for the New York City garment-workers' strike, 1913.

16. Funeral of the writer Shalom Aleichem in New York, 1916.

17. Dedication ceremonies, 1928, for Yeshiva University's original main building in Washington Heights.

17

Dreyfus
Affair

First Zionist
Congress

KISHINEV
POGROM

SECOND ALIYAH

British Mandate
Starts

BALFOUR DECLARATION

1880 1894 1897 1900 1903 1904 1910 1917 1920

Wright Brothers'
flight

Russo-Japanese
War

RUSSIAN REVOLUTION

BOER WAR

WORLD WAR I

20
Anti-Semitism
A Recurring Phenomenon

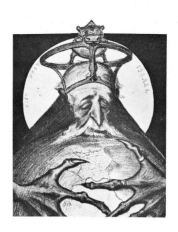

The conditions enjoyed by American Jewry were exceptional. Elsewhere Jewish communities entered a new period of trial. Those in the orient, as the Damascus Affair of 1840 showed, could still be accused of the most fantastic crimes. Those in Rumania still lived under the dark shadow of the cross. In both places, Jewish protests and international guarantees proved equally incapable of improving the situation fundamentally. But the numerous Jewish subjects of the Russian Czar were particularly unfortunate. Their numbers had been vastly increased by the partitions of Poland in the 18th century and the population explosion of the 19th. The majority were forced to live in a restricted Pale of Settlement. There they became the objects of popular hatred incited by the priests, and official discrimination imposed by reactionary governments. Amongst the range of special regulations designed to crush their spirit was the law that Jewish boys were to be conscripted into the Russian army for 25 years from the age of 12. Despite the vitality of Jewish life in the *shtetl*, Russian Jewry led a poverty-stricken and downtrodden existence. Only a sprinkling enriched themselves as large scale traders, bankers or railroad contractors.

Almost unbelievably, their conditions worsened after the brief liberal era initiated by Alexander II in 1855. For some years the discriminatory legislation was mitigated, and those Jews wishing to obtain a university education were encouraged to do so. But reaction soon regained the upper hand. In 1881, after a malicious rumor had been spread that Jews were responsible for the assassination of the Czar, pogroms were perpetrated throughout the Ukraine. This epidemic soon spread to Warsaw and Balta. The authorities, rather than seek the culprits, punished the victims. Such restrictions as those imposed by the infamous "May Laws" (1882) merely encouraged further popular excesses. The first year of the 20th century witnessed further massacres, particularly in Kishinev (1903) and Odessa (1905), which were often organized by police functionaries. The liberal experiment begun in 1905 did not reverse this trend. In 1913, the government concocted a Blood Libel trial in Kiev, accusing Mendel Beilis, a Jew, of murdering a Christian child for ritual purposes. These conditions accounted for the high proportion of Jews amongst the leadership of the various Russian revolutionary parties.

In the various European states to the west of the Russian border conditions, although less violent, were equally ominous. Despite their formal emancipation and economic success in these countries, the Jews had not won social acceptance. Neither had they shaken off their baneful medieval image of a group of Christ killers, blood suckers, and anti-patriotic aliens. Indeed in the wave of nationalism which swept Europe during the 19th century, the latter accusation became particularly strident. Admittedly, they were no longer discriminated against on denominational grounds. Instead, there gradually emerged a racist theory which postulated the division of mankind into "good" (i.e., gentile) and "bad" (i.e., Jewish) breeds. The new terminology was used as a cover for the old prejudices by left wing radicals no less than reactionary conservatives. Indeed the yellow press merely popularized the stereotype in the very countries in which elementary education was most widespread.

The new craze of anti-Semitism first attained serious proportions in Germany—where the term itself was coined in 1879 by an apostate Jew. There, the extent of popular prejudice had been revealed as early as the "Hep! Hep!" riots of 1819. A torrent of pseudo-scientific trash later fanned the flames. The Kaiser's own court preacher, Adolf Stoecker, founded a Christian Socialist Workingman's Union, which united the aristocracy, bourgeoisie, and proletariat in its anti-Jewish hate. But it was in France, the supposed home of Liberty, that matters reached a head. In 1895 Alfred Dreyfus, an Alsatian Jew on the French general staff, was falsely accused of spying for the Germans. Although he was ultimately exonerated in 1906, his various trials and pardons had been accompanied by a wild anti-Jewish campaign in the press, the streets and the Chamber.

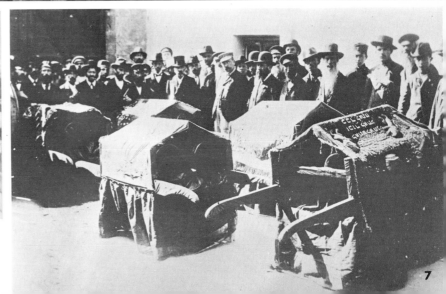

Motif: Rothschild in an anti-Semitic caricature by C. Léandre, 1898. This kind of theme was popularized by the frequent translation and publication of *The Protocols of the Learned Elders of Zion*, which first appeared during this period.

1. Torah scrolls in the Lemnoria Synagogue, desecrated in the Kishinev pogrom of 1903.

2. Ghost of Pharaoh warns Czar Alexander, whose boot rests on the neck of one of his Jewish subjects, and who is about to unsheath a sword labeled "Persecution": "Forebear! That weapon always wounds the hand that wields it." Cartoon in *Punch*, 1890.

3. Debris left after Kishinev pogrom, 1903. This was the pogrom that inspired some of Bialik's most impassioned poetry.

4. Kishinev family returns to its living room after the pogrom of 1903.

5. Some of the 67 Jews massacred in the pogrom at Yekaterinoslav, Ukraine, October 1905.

6. Secret meeting of a Bundist self-defense group in the woods near Pinsk, 1905.

7. Coffins for the burial of the Torah scrolls torn in the Kishinev pogrom of 1903. The biers are covered with embroidered curtains from the synagogue's Ark of the Law.

8. Dreyfus on trial. The blatant injustice of this farce and the evident helplessness of Diaspora Jewry aroused the active interest of an assimilated Viennese journalist who was covering the trial—Theodor Herzl.

9. Mastheads of Rumanian newspapers, 1899 and 1907.

10. Menahem Mendel Beilis escorted by guards to his trial in Kiev, 1913.

11. A 19th-century anti-Semitic motif is revived in *Zionism Unmasked*, a recent Arab publication.

ARAB RIOTS

3rd ALIYAH

ARAB RIOTS

4th ALIYAH

ARAB RIOTS

5th ALIYAH

1920 1921 1922 1923   1929 1930   1940

League of
Nations
started

End of
Ottoman
Empire

U.S.S.R. established

U.S.
Depression
starts

NAZISM

21

The Zionist Movement
The Early Pioneers

Amongst the observers of the Dreyfus trial was a Jewish journalist from Vienna, Theodor Herzl (1860-1904). Despite his almost totally assimilated background, Herzl was convinced by what he saw in Paris that anti-Semitism was an iradicable disease which he would escape only creating his own independent homeland. In 1895 he publicized his plan.

Herzl's call fell on ready ears. The continuity of Jewish life in Erez Israel had never been totally interrupted. Neither had the Diaspora relinquished its associations with that land. Ever since the Roman conquest of Judea, the dispersed Jews had retained the hope of returning there. This wish was constantly echoed in their prayers and ritual. Pilgrims regularly visited the Holy Land, while poets repeatedly recalled its past glories.

Recently these sentiments had begun to assume practical expression. In the 19th century such Orthodox rabbis as Zevi Hirsch Kalischer (1795-1874) and Judah Alkalai (1798-1878), had devised schemes for the Return and tried to raise the support necessary to implement them. Under the influence of European nationalism, their theories took an increasingly secular direction. The reconstruction of political nationhood in Palestine was advocated by a former assimilationist, the German Jewish thinker Moses Hess (1812-1875). It was also supported by such distinguished gentiles as the English authoress George Eliot. Their ideas became increasingly popular in the Russian Pale after the pogroms of 1881, when several nationalist societies and movements were formed in eastern Europe. Among the most important were the Hovevei Zion (Lovers of Zion) and the Bilu (a name taken from the Hebrew initials of the biblical verse "House of Jacob, come ye and let us go"). These groups even initiated a stream of emigration to Palestine, known as the First Aliyah (ascent). By the end of the 19th century they had established several ambitious, but not always commercially successful, agricultural colonies in that land.

Despite this wealth of existing inspiration, Herzl's contribution to the Zionist cause cannot be underestimated. His achievement was to make the movement universal; to provide it with leadership and organization; and to place it on the agenda of European diplomacy. Herzl aimed, not to increase the number of small colonies, but to fashion a complete state. To this end he convened biennial Zionist conferences of Jewish delegates from all over the globe (the first at Basle in 1897). He also created two financial institutions, the Jewish Colonial Trust and the Jewish National Fund, for furthering the movement's aims. Finally, he sought personal audiences with some of the most powerful crowned and elected heads of Europe. All this activity produced no immediate practical results. Herzl did not live to see the creation of the Jewish state; nor, even, did he win the unanimous support of his own people. His brand of political Zionism was opposed by many sectors of Jewry. The Orthodox feared to hasten the work best left to a time of God's own choosing; the assimilationists feared that his nationalistic trumpeting would endanger their own positions; and the socialists regarded his movement as a capitalist device.

Nevertheless, Herzl's instinct proved right. Under his charismatic leadership, the Zionist movement did gain an enormous following amongst the Jewish masses. The years after 1904 witnessed a second wave of *aliyah* to Erez Israel, and a remarkable renaissance of Hebrew language and literature there. Finally, and most important of all, the Zionist cause was in 1917 supported by a Great Power. As Herzl had foreseen, the reason was not idealistic but severely practical. The British government needed Jewish help in order to prevent Russia from leaving the war against Germany, and to strengthen America's resolve to come in. It also wished to use the Jews as a means of curtailing French influence in the Levant. Prompted by the efforts of Chaim Weizmann (1874-1952), Balfour, the British foreign secretary, accordingly promised to support "the establishment in Palestine of a national home for the Jewish people." After almost two thousand years Zion had again become a practical focus of Jewish hopes.

2

HARBINGER OF GOOD TIDINGS,

AN ADDRESS TO THE JEWISH NATION,

BY

RABBI JUDAH ELKALI.

ON THE PROPRIETY OF

ORGANIZING AN ASSOCIATION

TO PROMOTE THE

REGAINING OF THEIR FATHERLAND.

LONDON.
PUBLISHED BY S. SOLOMON, 37, DUKE STREET, ALDGATE.
5612.—1852.

[*Price Six Pence.*]

3

4

5

Fasse ich den Basler Congress
in ein Wort zusammen – das ich
mich hüten werde öffentlich aus-
zusprechen – so ist es dieses: in Basel
habe ich den Judenstaat gegründet.

Wenn ich das heute laut sagte, würde
mir ein universelles Gelächter ant-
worten. Vielleicht in fünf Jahren,
jedenfalls in fünfzig wird es Jeder
einsehen.

Foreign Office,
November 2nd, 1917.

Dear Lord Rothschild,

I have much pleasure in conveying to you, on behalf of His Majesty's Government, the following declaration of sympathy with Jewish Zionist aspirations which has been submitted to, and approved by, the Cabinet.

"His Majesty's Government view with favour the establishment in Palestine of a national home for the Jewish people, and will use their best endeavours to facilitate the achievement of this object, it being clearly understood that nothing shall be done which may prejudice the civil and religious rights of existing non-Jewish communities in Palestine, or the rights and political status enjoyed by Jews in any other country".

I should be grateful if you would bring this declaration to the knowledge of the Zionist Federation.

Motif: Herzl at Basle, depicted on stamp issued by Israel Post Office in 1960, the centenary of his birth.

1. Ḥalutzim at Gederah, Ereẓ Israel, 1913.

2. The emblem of the Bilu organization, incorporating a quotation from Isaiah.

3. Title page of a work by Judah Alkalai (1798–1878), Sephardi rabbi and a precursor of modern Zionism.

4. Ẓevi Hirsch Kalischer (1795–1874), Prussian rabbi who encouraged the growth of Jewish agriculture in Palestine.

5. The grave of Abraham Menahem Mendel Ussishkin (1863–1941), president of the Jewish National Fund, covered with bags of soil labeled with the names of the pioneering settlements whose land he had helped to acquire.

6. Reunion in 1922 of Bilu pioneers, celebrating 40th anniversary of founding of Rishon le-Zion.

7. Entrance of Mikveh Israel Agricultural School, founded in 1870 by the Alliance Israélite Universelle.

8. Training farm for ḥalutzim at Berdichev, the first in Russia, 1919.

9. Joseph Trumpeldor (1880–1920), who met his death defending the outpost of Tel Ḥai, and became a symbol of armed defense against Arab marauders.

10. Members of Hashomer defense group in Kefar Sava, 1911.

11. Aaronsohn family, pioneers of the Zikhron Ya'akov settlement, and founders of Nili, a pro-British underground organization during World War I.

12. Herzl leaving the Basle synagogue, 1903.

13. Entry in Herzl's diary, September 3, 1897, after the Congress: "At Basle I founded the Jewish state . . . Perhaps in five years, certainly in 50, everyone will realize it."

14. Herzl addressing the Second Congress, Basle, 1898.

15. Herzl's meeting with Kaiser Wilhelm II at Mikveh Israel, 1898, reconstructed in a contemporary photographic montage.

16. Kaiser Wilhelm II enters the Old City of Jerusalem, November 2, 1898.

17. Chaim Weizmann with the Emir Feisal at Aqaba, 1918.

18. Weizmann and Nahum Sokolow on either side of Lord Balfour, during the latter's visit to Ereẓ Israel in 1925.

19. The Balfour Declaration, November 2, 1917.

| | | | | | | | ALIYAH BET—ILLEGAL IMMIGRATION | | | | | | Peel Commission | | White Paper | | | | | | | | | Warsaw Ghetto Revolt | | | | Jewish Brigade | |

1933	1934	1935	1936	1937	1938	1939	1940	1941	1942	1943	1944	1945

New Deal · Nuremburg Laws · SPANISH CIVIL WAR · Pearl Harbor · W O R L D W A R I I · Atom Bomb

T H I R D R E I C H

22

The Final Solution
The Attempt at Genocide

1917 commenced a halycon period of hope in Europe, too. In that year Russian Jewry aquired full emancipation and the Pale of Settlement was abolished. Moreover, the minority rights guaranteed in 1919 by the Treaty of Versailles apparently assured the continuity of Jewish culture and identity throughout the newly-created "successor" states of central Europe. Everywhere, Jews participated in the work of post-war reconstruction with the same zest with which they had previously contributed to the war effort.

Once again, Jewish hopes proved unfounded. In Russia, the civil war and the process of forced agriculturalization wreaked havoc on Jewish life. Furthermore the Bolshevik regime, although it intermittently encouraged Yiddish culture, proved even more repressive than its czarist precursors. It forced the people of the Bible to accede to the writ of Marxist–Leninism and conducted a brutal campaign against Jewish culture, nationalism and worship. The Zionists and the Jewish Socialist Party (the Bund) tried, in their separate ways, to retain a constructive sense of Jewish identity. But their efforts were frustrated by popular anti-Semitism, itself exacerbated by chronic economic crisis. In America the Ku Klux Klan and in England the Blackshirts, also enjoyed some measure of support.

In defeated Germany anti-Semitism reached a violent peak of madness. Even before the advent to power of the Nazis, the supposed Jewish stranglehold on German life was blamed for every conceivable ill—Bolshevism, economic chaos and political crisis. Adolf Hitler, who became chancellor of Germany in 1933, transformed such feelings into official government policy. Hatred of the Jews was the one consistent element in his otherwise jumbled collection of ideas. Under Nazi direction, German newspapers disseminated racialist poison and the German people were encouraged to remove the Jewish excrement from the body politic. The Nuremburg Laws of May 1935 combined the barbarity of medieval legislation with the inhumanity of modern logic. They deprived the Jews (together with a new breed of "half-Jews") of citizenship, restricted their possibilities of employment, and curtailed their communal activities. Worse was still to come. On the 9th of November 1938 a nationwide pogrom was perpetrated; synagogues were gutted, Jews thrown into concentration camps and their businesses looted. Despite the immigration restrictions imposed by almost every European country, considerable numbers of German Jews managed to escape this hell. Those who remained even fashioned something of a cultural revival. But long before 1939 it was clear that the cradle of Ashkenazi Jewry was being destroyed.

The extension of Nazi power to other European countries before and during World War II served to widen and intensify the brutal effects of anti-Semitism. Each German victory—a series unbroken until the end of 1942—spelled immediate horror for the Jews who came under Nazi rule. From France to the Ukraine the Nazis abetted popular outrages and organized criminal violence. They employed an unvarying compound of deception, cruelty and psychological pressure to dehumanize the Jews. They then deported them to concentration camps. There the victims were subject to a constant and worsening situation of hunger, epidemics and torture. In accordance with the Final Solution, ultimately formulated in 1942, they were also condemned to fiendish death. By the time the Nazis had been defeated between four and a half and six million Jews had been massacred.

Despite this satanic trial the Jewish spirit was not completely broken. Several Jewish uprisings took place in the ghettos and concentration camps, notably Warsaw and Treblinka. Jewish partisans operated whenever they could find shelter, which was often denied to them by their non-Jewish comrades in arms. But even those who somehow managed to retain their belief in God, had lost much of their faith in mankind. The horrors of the Holocaust were perpetrated, not despite modern civilization, but largely with the aid of mass culture, mass education and the use of mass media for propaganda and indoctrinization.

Deutsche, verteidigt Euch
gegen die jüdische
Greuelpropaganda,
kauft
nur bei Deutschen!

Germans defend
yourselves against jewish
atrocity propaganda
buy only at German shops!

ACHTUNG
JUDEN

Motif: Train to extermination camp; woodcut by Moshe Hoffman.

1. Electrified fence surrounding Auschwitz.

2-3-4-5. Eastern Europe Between the Wars.

2. Habimah performance of S. An-Ski's *The Dybbuk*, Moscow, 1922.

3. A street in the Jewish settlement project at Birobidzhan in the early 1930s.

4. Settlers read Yiddish newspaper at the Jewish collective farm at Stalindorf, Ukraine, late 1930s.

5. Typical group of Jewish orphans found roaming about Eastern Europe after World War I.

6-11. The Rise of Nazism.

6. Nazi Party mass rally in Nuremberg, 1933.

7. Adolf Hitler.

8. The "New Order."

9. Nazis picketing Jewish shops.

10. Propaganda posters, c. 1938.

11. Destruction of Jewish shops, November, 1938.

12-20. The Final Solution.

12. Transport of women and children arrives at Auschwitz. The Jewish badge is a medieval revival.

13. The burning of books (May 10, 1933); another medieval tactic revived.

14. Jews forced to ride each other; Minsk, 1941.

15. Auschwitz inmates who committed suicide by hurling themselves against the high-voltage fence.

16. Jews executed in Lodz, Poland.

17. Women, children, and babes in arms await their death; Poland, c. 1941.

18. Women S.S. guards at Bergen Belsen camp forced by the British to bury their victims.

19. Mass execution; photograph taken from a German prisoner of war.

20. S.S. men amuse themselves by kicking a Jew; Poland, c. 1939–40.

21. Heroic defiance expressed in the memorial sculpture by Nathan Rapaport on the site of the Warsaw Ghetto uprising.

לב אברהם וזכרי
24.3.1948

British Mandate Ends
ISRAEL STATEHOOD
WAR OF INDEPENDENCE
Rhodes Armistice
Weizmann President
BEN-GURION PRIME MINISTER
Ben-Zvi President
SHARETT PRIME MINISTER

1945	1946	1947	1948	1949	1950	1951	1952	1953	1954	1955

U.N.
General Assembly

INDIA
PAKISTAN
INDEPENDENT

Berlin Blockade

COMMUNIST CHINA

NATO

NASSER ASSUMES CONTROL

KOREAN WAR

23

The Struggle for Statehood
Determination and Sacrifice

Jewish life in Ereẓ Israel between the wars had also proved difficult. In particular, Arab nationalism—the sentiment which the early Zionists had tended to discount—fostered attacks on the Jews and their enterprises. In a series of violent outbreaks (1921, 1929, 1933, and 1936-38), the Arabs tried to break Jewish morale and to blackmail the British mandatory authorities into curtailing *aliyah*. In consequence Jewish immigration was indeed limited by various criteria and formalities, and was further restricted by the particularly harsh White Paper of 1939.

Nevertheless the *yishuv* (meaning settlement) made remarkable progress, becoming a source of pride to the faithful and wonder to the skeptics. A national structure was formed with the establishment in 1920 of the *Va'ad Leummi* (National Council) and the modern Chief Rabbinate. Considerable tracts of neglected land were acquired, and in many cases were colonized by a novel form of voluntary agricultural collective (kibbutz). Sixty eight of these had been established before 1939. Meanwhile, Jewish suburbs outside the cities of Jerusalem and Tel Aviv developed with amazing rapidity. Moreover, and true to Jewish tradition, material progress was accompanied by intellectual achievement. The pioneers developed a rich cultural (and in some cases spiritual) life, establishing Hebrew printing houses, theaters and a University. These trends were accelerated during the 1930s by a wave of immigration from central Europe. The skill, abilities and money of German Jews in particular did much to develop industry and advance technology. They also increased the country's absorptive capacity. Its Jewish population rose from under 40,000 in 1920 to over half a million in 1939.

Meanwhile, the Zionists also took steps to ensure their physical safety. In 1921 a clandestine security organization known as the Haganah was formed. It developed an underground system of training, arms hoarding and tactics and a striking force known as the Palmaḥ. It was initially designed to cope with the problem of Arab outbreaks but also endeavored to help "illegal" immigrants circumvent restrictions imposed by the British authorities. Nevertheless, and in contrast to the attitude adopted by most Arabs, over 40,000 Palestinian Jews served in the British Army during the war against Hitler. After 1945, however, they intensified their efforts to save the remnant of European Jewry by illegal immigration. The Zionist politicians, meanwhile, decided to win independence. They had been willing to negotiate the limited offer made by the Peel Commission in 1937 (which the Arab higher committee rejected); in 1942 they adopted the Biltmore program calling for a Jewish state.

After 1945 the *yishuv* thus fought simultaneously on three fronts. One battle was against the British policy of limited immigration—most pointedly expressed in the fate of the refugee ship *Exodus* in 1947. This struggle took the form of terrorist activity, especially by the *Irgun Ẓevai Leummi* and *Loḥamei Ḥerut Israel*. After a period of rising tension and violence, the British government in 1947 referred the problem to the United Nations. There was waged the second struggle, that for international recognition of the Jewish right to statehood in Palestine. This reached a climax on November 29, 1947, when the general assembly prodded jointly by the U.S.A. and Russia, voted to establish separate Jewish and Arab states there. On May 14, 1948, David Ben Gurion proclaimed the establishment of the State of Israel.

Even before then however, the *yishuv* had begun to face its third test—that of physical survival. In 1947 the Arab states declared their determined opposition to the United Nations resolution, and instigated murderous assaults on Jewish traffic and settlements. In May 1948 their regular armies invaded the infant Jewish state, thus forcing it into a war of independence. Despite their inferiority in numbers and equipment, the Israelis managed to defend most of their existing places of settlement (the Jewish quarter of East Jerusalem being a tragic exception) and even to extend the borders alloted to them. Hostilities did not finally cease until the Rhodes armistice agreements between Israel and her neighbors in 1949.

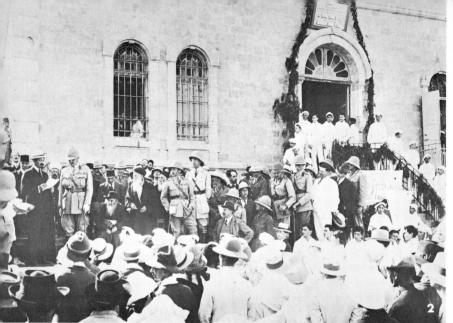

126

127

12

13

14

15

17

Motif: Stockade and watchtower, symbol of pioneering settlement in Ereẓ Israel between 1936 and 1947. In all, 118 such settlements were established in various parts of the country in planned surprise operations which in the course of one day provided immediate security against Arab attacks.

1. These armored vehicles opened the road to beleaguered Jerusalem in 1948; their burnt-out chassis have been left by the roadside as a memorial.
2. Weizmann presents General Allenby with a Torah scroll; Jerusalem, 1918.
3. *Ḥalutzot* of the Third Aliyah build the Afulah-Nazareth road, c. 1920.
4. Camels make their way down Allenby Street, Tel Aviv, early 1920s.
5. Lord Balfour, flanked by civic and religious dignitaries from Ereẓ Israel and abroad, opens the Hebrew University at Mount Scopus; April 1, 1925.
6. Desecration of the Great Sephardi Synagogue "Avraham Avinu," Hebron, 1929.
7. Youth Aliyah wards from Germany on their arrival in Ereẓ Israel, c. 1933.
8. "They that sow in tears shall reap in joy" (Ps. 126:5); *ḥalutzim* in 1935.
9. Stockade and watchtower settlement at Nir David, 1936.
10. Arab rioters in Jaffa, 1936.
11. The Round Table Conference of 1939 at St. James Palace, London. Since the Arab delegates refused to sit together with the Jews, the Conference was held in two separate sessions.
12. "Illegal" immigrants disembark from the *Parita*; Tel Aviv, August 1939.
13. The *Exodus 1947* after the conflict between the Haganah and the British.
14. Interrogation and search for arms at kibbutz Sedot Yam, 1946.
15. The last deported "illegal" immigrants leave the Cyprus detention camp, February 11, 1949.
16. Water tower at Be'erot Yiẓḥak; August 1948.
17. Headlines of *The Palestine Post*, May 16, 1948.
18. British soldiers in Jerusalem pack their belongings, May 13/14, 1948.

SINAI CAMPAIGN

——————BEN-GURION PRIME MINISTER——————

Eichmann Trial

RUMANIAN
ALIYAH

Shazar President

——————ESHKOL PRIME MINISTER——

| 1955 | 1956 | 1957 | 1958 | 1959 | 1960 | 1961 | 1962 | 1963 | 1964 | 1965 |

| | Hungarian Revolt | SPUTNIK I | De Gaulle elected | Castro Premier of Cuba | Congo Crisis | First Man in Space | Cuban Crisis | Kennedy Assassinated | | U.S. offensive in Vietnam |
| | | | | | | Berlin Wall | ALGERIA INDEPENDENT | | | |

24
The State of Israel
A Quarter Century of Progress

From its foundation, the State of Israel has granted citizenship to every Jew wishing to live there. The earliest arrivals included survivors of the Holocaust, from the displaced persons camps of Europe and Cyprus. They were followed by an influx of refugees from Arab lands and by less numerous immigrants from western countries. Immigration from the United States increased after 1967 and significant numbers of Soviet Jews arrived after 1971. By 1974, the Jewish population had grown from some 650,000 to almost three million. Many of the immigrants, especially those of oriental extraction, were poor and unskilled. They periodically protested against discrimination by the predominantly Ashkenazi establishment.

In spite of the burdens imposed by immigration, the country experienced a period of rapid economic growth, helped in some measure by reparations from Germany and aid from the United States. Within 25 years the state doubled its industrial output, trebled the area under cultivation, quintupled its exports and became almost self-supporting in staple foodstuffs. Despite a recession from 1965 to 1967 the gross national production rose by ten to 11 percent, causing serious inflationary pressures.

Israel also became a stable parliamentary democracy. Elections to the 120-member Knesset (parliament) were first held in January 1949. In these, and in the six subsequent general elections, the Labor Party emerged as the dominant coalition partner. It has adopted a socialist program, instituting free, compulsory primary education and welfare schemes. Higher education and scientific research were also encouraged, and Israel contains seven institutions of higher learning. The Arab citizens of Israel possess equal rights and elect representatives to the Knesset.

Israel has maintained close ties with the Diaspora. World Jewry supported the state by providing large-scale funds, as well as Israel bonds to the value of one and a half billion dollars between 1951 and 1970. Jewish "lobbies" have also tried to create the climate favorable to Israel in the western democracies. In turn, Israel has become something of a spiritual center for the Jewish world. The Jewish Agency regularly dispatches emissaries to the Diaspora, where they contribute to the continuity and deepening of Hebrew and Jewish culture. Nevertheless religious problems, particularly the definition of Jewish identity for registration purposes, have sometimes strained relations between the Israel Rabbinate and Progressive congregations in the United States. The trial and execution of Eichmann (1961-62) gave Israel-born youth a new insight into the Holocaust.

The problem of security has dominated Israel's history. The Arab states have persistently refused to sign peace treaties with Israel, declaring the continuity of their struggle against her. Initially, this took the form of an international economic boycott and a refusal to allow Israeli ships passage through the Suez Canal. Increasingly, they turned to armed conflict. They encouraged resistance amongst Palestinian refugees who had fled during the War of Independence and who were not re-settled in Arab lands. By 1956, armed infiltrators had caused several hundred Israeli civilian deaths. They also formed a joint Arab military command led by Nasser's Egypt. In October 1956, Israel reacted by joining an Anglo-French invasion of Egypt and occupied the Gaza Strip and Sinai. A UN peacekeeping force subsequently established a temporary truce. But in 1967 the Arab states, with Soviet backing, again threatened Israel's existence. In a lightning campaign (the Six-Day War) the Israel army routed the combined forces of Egypt, Jordan, Syria and Iraq, reunited Jerusalem, and pushed back the Arab threat from Israel's population centers. But despite the liberal regime adopted in the Israel-held territories, the political problems remained unsolved. Between 1967 and 1972, Israeli citizens were faced with a terrorist campaign both within and without the country, and a war of attrition across the Suez Canal. On the Day of Atonement 1973 they were suddenly attacked by Egypt and Syria. After three weeks of severe battle and a further period of intense negotiation, a partial settlement was reached with Egypt.

132

134

Motif: Israel defends, cultivates and rejoices; Independence Day poster, 1965.

1-2. The stricken exiles return to the Land of Promise.

3-8. From the Four Corners of the Earth.

3. Yemenites in Operation Magic Carpet, 1949.

4. Displaced Persons arrive in Israel, January 1949.

5. Georgian migrants in Jerusalem, 1972.

6. Rumanian family reunites; Haifa, 1959.

7. Migrant absorption center at Nazareth, 1968.

8. Migrant absorption center, 1953; floods in temporary *ma'abarah* quarters.

9-14. Not by Bread Alone.

9. Yehudi and Hephzibah Menuhin at military hospital, April 1950.

10. "A Psalm of David," rendition by Inbal dance troupe.

11. Buying and browsing at the annual Hebrew Book Week.

12. Courtyard of the Rockefeller Archaeological Museum.

13. Yaakov Agam exhibition, Tel Aviv Museum.

14. Sophocles in modern Greek at Roman amphitheater, Caesarea.

15-21. People of the Book.

15. Conferment of doctorates at Hebrew University, Mount Scopus.

16. Tel Aviv campus of Bar Ilan, a religious university.

17. Weizmann Institute of Science, Rehovot.

18. Negev Institute for Arid Zone Research, Beersheba; measuring solar radiation.

19. Jerusalem College for Women; class in biblical exegesis.

20. Talmud study at Yeshivat Mercaz ha-Rav, Jerusalem.

21. Fishery school at Mevo'ot Yam.

22-27. But by My Spirit.

22. Mosque of Ahmad Jazzar Pasha, Acre.

23. Dancing in street with Torah scrolls, Tel Aviv.

24. Chief Rabbi Unterman addresses Christian and Muslim dignitaries in reunited Jerusalem, June 27, 1967; presiding is prime minister Levi Eshkol.

25. Church of the Nativity, Bethlehem.

26. Gold-domed Bahai temple, Haifa.

27. Druze leaders in traditional dress.

28-34. Pray for the Peace of Jerusalem.

28. Tel Aviv bus station after bombing, 1949.

29. Weapons abandoned by Egyptians, Sinai Campaign, 1956.

30. Dwelling at kibbutz Gadot, Eastern Upper Galilee, after shelling from Golan Heights, April 1967.

31. Nasser closes the Straits of Tiran, while Iraq, Lebanon and Syria stand ready; from *Al Jarida*, May 25, 1967.

32. The Western Wall liberated, June 7, 1967.

33. Reservist on pontoon bridge spanning Suez Canal, October 1973.

34. Improvised *sukkah* atop half-track in Golan Heights, October 1973.

35-39. People and Events.

35. Ben-Gurion addresses Provisional Council, May 14, 1948.

36. Filmed documentation at Eichmann trial, June 1961.

37. Prime minister Golda Meir addresses Knesset, November 1973.

38. Zalman Shazar, president of Israel, 1963-73.

39. Demonstration of solidarity with Soviet Jewry, December 1970.

Agnon receives
Nobel Prize   SIX-DAY WAR   WAR OF ATTRITION   GOLDA MEIR PRIME MINISTER
                                        RUSSIAN ALIYAH   YOM KIPPUR WAR
                                                                              Katzir President

1966   1967   1968   1969   1970   1971   1972   1973   1974

First Heart Transplant   Czechoslovakian
                                    invasion   Man on Moon   Communist China
                                                                                  admitted to U.N.

25

World Jewry in the 1970s
An Unbroken Chain

For a considerable proportion of the Jewish people, the existence of the State of Israel marks a watershed in Jewish history. It has proved the fulfillment of their dreams and has provided a creative center of Jewish culture. Israel has also become a focus of Jewish fears. The tense atmosphere in the Diaspora during moments of danger to the State indicate the extent to which many Jews outside Israel feel their own fate and welfare to be bound up with that of the independent Jewish country.

But Israel is not the only center of Jewish life. Indeed, the role which American Jewry, in particular, now plays in the development of Jewish culture has been compared with that of Hellenistic Alexandria, ancient Babylon and medieval Spain. It is in the United States that some of the greatest contributions to Jewish literature, history and art are being made; there that Reform Judaism (the Union of American Hebrew Congregations celebrated its centenary in 1973) has become a vital force; and there that the Conservative movement has flourished. Together with these new trends, such traditional groups as the Ḥasidim and the Orthodox synagogues have also flowered. These cultural achievements have been matched by the extraordinary social and political progress. The influence which the Jews as a group are able to exert on the nation's political and commercial life is equalled only by the contribution which Jews as individuals have made to its artistic and scientific progress.

This pattern is paralleled, although by no means equalled, elsewhere in the western world. The Jewish communities of England, South-Africa, Canada, western Europe and Latin America have also taken full advantage of the coincidence of civic liberties and economic opportunities. There too the number of Jews in the professions is continually rising and their position in society is beginning to look increasingly secure. In each of these countries Jews sit in the national parliament, are represented by well-organized communal institutions, and support their own programs of social welfare and religious education.

Nevertheless the picture is not uniformly comforting. Many of the old dangers remain and several new perils have come to the fore. Despite the efforts of Pope John XXIII, the old Christian attitude towards the Jews has not totally changed. Moreover, since the war, the phenomenon of anti-Semitism has occasionally reappeared in Germany, while Arab propaganda against Israel has revived some of its worst features. Even in the United States Jews are facing an imponderable problem from without in the emergence of "black" anti-Semitism amongst negro society. World Jewry also faces criticism and desertion from within. Some groups show strong manifestations of Jewish "self-hate"—particularly intellectuals of the new Left—often in the guise of anti-Zionism. Others show an increasing propensity towards mixed marriages with gentiles. As a result, several Jewish communities in Europe and America face a state of acute demographic and cultural crisis.

The vast Jewish community of Soviet Russia faces the greatest problem of all. After a brief period of Israel-Soviet cordiality, relations between the two states worsened and Jewish citizens of Russia have been subjected to a steady stream of discriminatory practices, cultural deprivation and verbal abuse. Nevertheless, significant numbers of Soviet Jews have continued to evince determined efforts to win their freedom. In particular, some have courageously demanded the right to emigrate to Israel. Despite the legal charges to which such applications have sometimes given rise and the exorbitant exit fees imposed by the Soviet authorities, this pressure has been unabating. In 1972 a record number of 30,000 Jews left the U.S.S.R. for Israel.

Moreover, the struggle for Soviet Jewish rights has become one of the focal phenomena in Jewish life the world over; the redemption of Soviet Jewry is now a central challenge for the entire Jewish people. The issue has thus become a reflection of all Jewish history. Indeed it is in that story that Jews find eternal comfort. It teaches that the Jewish spirit will continue to survive, whatever the uncertainties of the future and the tribulations of the present.

2

3

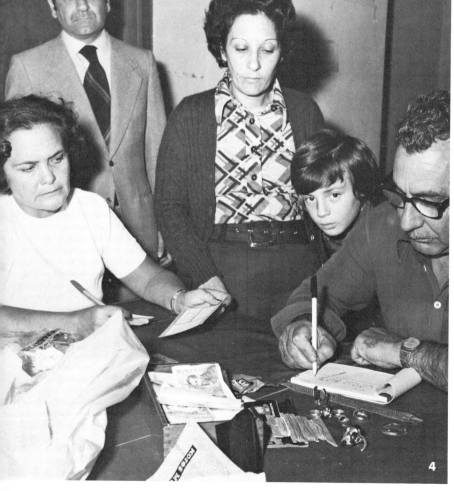

4

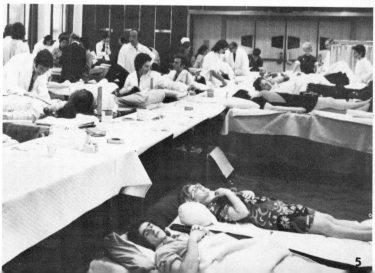

5

141

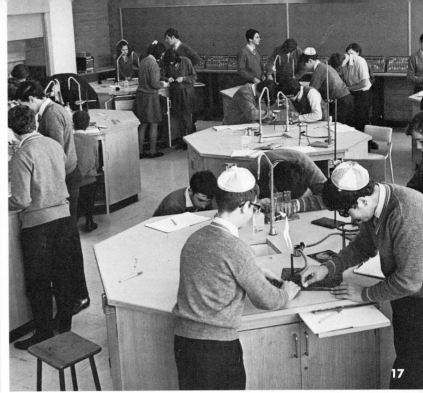

Motif: "Israel, I love you;" Belgian lapel pin, October 1973.

1. Pro-Israel demonstration in Paris, October 1973.

2-5. When we Remembered Zion.

2. Fundraising bazaar of Tokyo's Jewish community, December 1973, opened by Princess Chichibu.

3. South African volunteers arrive at Tel Aviv, November 1973.

4. Rome's Jews contribute jewelry to Israel's war effort, October 1973.

5. Anglo-Jewish blood donors in St. John's Wood Synagogue.

6-11. Life in the New World.

6. Kosher meat and motion pictures; Beverly Hills, L.A.

7. City of Hope, California; nonsectarian philanthropy under Jewish auspices.

8. Civil rights march, Alabama, 1965; Abraham Joshua Heschel (right) with Martin Luther King.

9. Camp Morasha, community service project of Yeshiva University.

10. Vigilante motor patrol, Brooklyn, 1964.

11. Israel Day parade, New York, 1971.

12-18. To Sing the Lord's Song on Alien Soil.

12. Berlin's new Fasanenstrasse synagogue incorporates elements of the prewar edifice destroyed by the Nazis.

13. Carmel College Synagogue, Berkshire, England; stained-glass windows designed by Nehemiah Azzaz and executed by pupils.

14. Jewish Lads' Pipe Brigade, Glasgow, Scotland.

15. Their brothers' keeper; demonstration in London, 1972.

16. Moscow yeshivah, 1973.

17. Chemistry class at Mt. Scopus College, Melbourne, Australia.

18. Traditional motifs in contemporary garb; Expo '67, Montreal.

Illustration Credits

Israel Dept. of Antiquities & Museums, 1:1, 2, 3; 2:4; 4: motif, 6; 7:2, 4; 8:2; 10:5.

Hebrew University, Institute of Archaeology, Jerusalem, 1:2.

J.N.U.L., 1:4, 2:2; 6:7; 10: motif; 11: motif; 16: motif, 4; 17:4, 11; 20:1, 3, 5, 7; 23:17; Schwadron Coll., 17:2, 6, 7, 9, 10; 10:16; 21:3, 10, 18; Photo Coll., 18:1; 20:4.

Fratelli Alinari, Florence, 1:5, 7; 3:4; 4:1.

The Cleveland Museum of Art, Mr. and Mrs. William H. Marlatt Fund, 1:6.

W. Flinders Petrie, *Six Temples at Thebes*, London, 1890, plate 8, 1:8.

Austrian National Library Photo Archives, Vienna, 1:9.

National Gallery of Art, Washington, D.C., Andrew Mellon Collection, 1:11.

Sarajevo National Museum, p. 65.

Yale University, New Haven, Conn., 1:12; 3:2; 5:3; 11:2.

The British Library Board, London, 2: motif; 3: motif; 4:5; 21:19; p. 66 (left).

Moshe Levine, *Mlekhet ha-Mishkan*, Tel Aviv, 1968, 2:3.

Israel Museum, 6:13; 9:2, 13; 12:4, 6, 7; 14:4; 15:2; 16:5; 17:3; 18:2, 4; p. 67 (below); p. 72 (below l.); p. 78 (all except above l.); p. 79 (center and r.); Bronfman Archaeological Museum, 2:5; 6:1, 3; Dept. of Ethnography, Photo Shulman, 12:13.

Kunsthistorisches Museum, Vienna, 2:6.

Israel Government Press Office, Tel Aviv, 2:7; 6:8; 7:3; 8: motif, 6, 7; 9:1; 10:1, 6; 11:1; 14:9; 16:1; 21:7, 23:1, 16; 24:motif, 3, 4, 5, 7, 9, 11–15, 18, 21–30, 35–39.

Prado Museum, Madrid, 3:1.

Royal Picture Gallery, Mauritshuis, The Hague, Photo A. Dingjan, 3:3.

Encyclopaedia of Archaeological Excavations in the Holy Land, Ramat Gan, 1970, 3:5.

After Y. Aharoni, *Carta's Atlas of the Bible*, 3:6.

Royal Museum of Fine Arts, Copenhagen, 3:7.

Basle, Kunstmuseum, Dept. of Prints and Drawings, 4:2.

Amiens, Bibliothèque Municipale, Ms. 108 fol. 106v, 4:3.

Library of San Isidoro, Leon, Spain, 4:4.

Bibliothèque Nationale, 4:8; 6:9.

Central Zionist Archives, 4:7; 6:5; 20:8, 21:1, 4, 6, 8, 12, 13, 14, 15, 16, 17; 23:3, 11, 15.

Persia, The Immortal Kingdom, Photos by MacQuilty, 5: motif, 5.

Photo Peter Larsen, Jerusalem, 5:1, 6; 9:5.

The Brooklyn Museum, Bequest of Miss Theodora Wilbour, 5:2.

Formerly Charles Feinberg Collection, Detroit, Photo Manning Brothers, 5:4.

Library of the Armenian Patriarchate, Jerusalem, 5:7.

Photo David Harris, Jerusalem, 5:8; 6:13; 9:13; 13:motif; 15:2; 8:4; p. 67 (below); p. 68; p. 70 (above); p. 73; p. 75 (above and below); p. 76 (below); p. 78; p. 79.

S. A. Birnbaum, *The Hebrew Scripts*, London, 1954–7, 6: motif.

University Library, University of Michigan, Ann Arbor, Michigan, 6:2.

Keren Hayesod, United Jewish Appeal Photo Archives, 6:4; 23:12; 13:14; 24:6, 8.

Album ha-Olim, Tel Aviv, 1965, 6:6; 24:2.

The Archbishop of Canterbury and the Trustees of Lambeth Palace Library, 6:10.

Rome, Vatican Library, 6:11; 15:8.

Société de Jésus, Provenance de Paris, 6:12.

The Jewish Museum, New York, 6:14.

The Jewish Museum, London, Photo Warburg Institute, 6:15.

Landesbildstelle, Berlin, 6:16; 25:12.

Leipzig University, *Gesamtkatalog der Wiegendrucke*, 1925–8, 4307–8, 7: motif.

Bibliothèque Municipale, Dijon, France, 7:1.

J.-B. Frey, *Corpus Inscriptionum Judaicarum*, Vol. I, 1936, 7:5.

Photo Zev Radovan, Jerusalem, 7:6; 9:9; 10:7; 13:6.

Musée de Cluny, Paris, 7:7.

Photo Werner Braun, Jerusalem, 8:1, 4, 5, 8; 9:4; 12:2; 24:16, 17, 19, 20, 32; p. 69 (below); p. 72 (above right); p. 74; p. 77 (above right and below left).

Israel Exploration Society, Jerusalem, 8:3.

Courtesy Yigael Yadin, Jerusalem, 8:4; 9:8, 9.

Coins of Erez Israel, Bank of Israel Collection, Jerusalem, 1971, 9:6, 12.

Sir Charles Wilson (ed.) *Picturesque Palestine, Sinai and Egypt*, London, c. 1880, 9:7.

National Parks Authority, Tel Aviv, 9:10.

Jewish Theological Seminary of America, 10:2; 19: motif (Photo Frank Darmstaedter).

Library of the Hungarian Academy of Sciences, Budapest, Kaufmann Collection, 10:3.

Photo Yizhak Amit, Kibbutz Zora, 10:4.

Staatliche Museum, Fruechristlich-byzantinische Sammlung, Berlin, 11:2.

Academy Photo Offset Inc., New York, 11:4.

Photo K. Weiss, Jerusalem, 11:6, 7.

The Chester Beatty Library, Dublin, 12: motif.

American Jewish Joint Distribution Committee, 12:1; 22:5.

Izhak Einhorn Collection, Tel Aviv, 13: motif.

J. Caro Baroja, *Los Judicos en la Espana Moderna y Contemporanea*, Madrid, 1961, 13:2.

The Jewish Chronicle, London 13:4; 25:5 (Photo Peter Fisher).

Photo Alfred Rubens, London, 13:5.

Photo Heliotipa Artistica Espanola, Madrid, 13:8.

Rijksmuseum, Amsterdam, 13:9.

Photo M. Ninio, Jerusalem, 13:10.

Cecil Roth Coll., 13:13; 15:5; 18:3, 8, 9; p. 69 (below); p. 78 (above l.); p. 79 (r.).

Stadtische Kulturinstitute, Worms, 14:2, 5; p. 72 (above left).

Z. Asaria, *Die Juden in Koln*, Cologne, 1959, 14:3.

Koblenz, Staatarchiv Rheinland–Pfalz, 14:6.

Mittelrheinisches Museum, Mainz, 14:7.

Central Archives for the History of the Jewish People, Jerusalem, 14:8 (Rh/w, Ai); 22:3.

Photo Bernard Biraben, Bordeaux, 14:10, 11.

Soprintendenza alle Gallerie Gabinetto Fotografico, Firenze, 14:13, 16.

Yad Veshem, 14:15; 15:9 (Y. D. Kamson Coll.), 22:1, 8–12, 15–17, 20; p. 75 (above).

George Lukomski, *Old European Synagogues*, 15: motif.

Mishkan le-Omanut Museum of Art, Ein Harod, 15:1, 3, 6; p. 72 (below right).

M. Balaban, *Historja Zydow w Krakowie*, 1936, 15:4.

Oscar Gruss Collection, New York, 15:7; 16:8 (Photo Frank Darmstaedter).

Milan, Biblioteca Ambrosiana, 16:2.

Library of Congress, Washington, 16:3.

Jewish National Fund, Jerusalem, 16:7; 21:5; 23:7, 9; 24:1; p. 70 (below).

Photo David Eisenberg, Jerusalem, 16:11.

Photo David Posner, Jerusalem, 16:12; 25:6.

Nuremberg, Germanisches Nationalmuseum, 17: motif.

Union of American Hebrew Congregations, New York, 17:1.

J. Michman (Melkman) Photo Collection, Jerusalem, 17:5.

Berlin, Nationalgalerie, Staatliche Museum Preussischer Kulturbesitz, 17:8.

Daniel M. Friedenberg Collection, New York, 18:5.

J. C. Ulrichs, *Sammlung juedischer Geschichten . . . in der Schweitz*, Basle, 1765, 18:6.

The Bettman Archive, New York, 19:1.

Staten Island Historical Society, Richmondtown, 19:2 (Photo Alice Austen).

Utah State Historical Society, Salt Lake City, 19:3.

Amador County Museum, photocopy by Al Fugett Studio, Jackson, 19:4.

American Jewish Historical Society, Waltham, Mass., 19:5, 9.

American Jewish Archive of the Hebrew Union College, 19:6.

U.P.I., New York, 19:7, 15; 25:10.

H. Hapgood, *Spirit of the Ghetto*, Belknap Press, Harvard University Press, 19:10, 11.

Frank Simon and A. Feininger, *New York*, London, 1964, 19:12.

Morris U. Schappes, *The Jews in the United States*, New York, 1958, 19:14.

E. Fuchs, *Die Juden in der Karikatur*, 1921, 20: motif.

Bund Archives of the Jewish Labor Movement, New York, 20:6.

YIVO, Institute of Jewish Studies, New York, 20:10.

A. Rafaeli-Zenziper, Archive for Russian Zionism, Tel Aviv, 21:2; 22:2.

Haganah Historical Archives, Tel Aviv, 21:9; 23:10.

Beit Aaronsohn, Zikhron Yaakov, 21:11.

Rina Gallery (Mrs. Bertha Urdang), Jerusalem, 20: motif.

Z. Efron Collection, Ein Harod, 22:4.

Courtesy Shaefer Verlag, Munich, 22:6.

Photo Ullstein, Berlin, 22:13.

Courtesy Leib Rochman, Jerusalem, 22:14.

Imperial War Museum, London, 22:18.

Israel State Archives, Jerusalem, 23:2, 5.

Haarez Museum of the History of Tel Aviv–Yafo, Photo A. Soskin, 23:4.

Photo Yaakov Benor–Kalter, *Photographs of the New Working Palestine*, 1935, 23:8.

Jerusalem Municipality Historical Archives, 23:18.

Photo Keren-Kidron, Tel Aviv, 24:10.

Photo Mike Goldberg, Neveh Ilan, 24:34.

Rabbi Tokayer, Tokyo, 25:2.

I.P.P.A., Tel Aviv, 25:3.

Chief Rabbi Toaff, Photo Marcello Maggiori, Rome, 25:4.

Photo Herbert Sonnenfeld, N.Y., 25:9.

Photo by Archer Associates, N.Y., 25:11.

Jewish Lads Brigade, Glasgow, Photo A. W. Middlemiss, 25:14.

Press Service, Tel Aviv, 25:15.

Photo Jesse Zel Lurie, N.Y., 25:16.

Photo Allan Studios, Collingwood, Australia, 25:17.

Briston Films Ltd., Montreal, 25:18.

William Margulies Collection, London, p. 66 (right)

Photo Richard Cleave, p. 67 (above).

Sir Isaac and Lady Wolfson Museum in Hechal Shlomo, Jerusalem, p. 73.

Photo David Rubinger, Jerusalem, p. 76 (above).

Photo Murray Bloom, Jerusalem, p. 77 (above left).